Prison Patter

A Dictionary of Prison Words and Slang

Angela Devlin is the author of the acclaimed *Criminal Classes* (Waterside Press, 1995) which examines the links between educational failure and later offending behaviour. She became interested in prison language when interviewing prisoners for that book and while conducting further research in women's prisons.

D1598909

Wombling

Prison Patter

A Dictionary of Prison Words and Slang

Angela Devlin

Illustrated by Maryanne

WATERSIDE PRESS
WINCHESTER

Prison Patter
A Dictionary of Prison Words and Slang

Published 1996 by
WATERSIDE PRESS
Domum Road
Winchester SO23 9NN
Telephone or Fax 01962 855567
INTERNET:106025.1020@compuserve.com

ISBN Paperback 1 872 870 41 4

Cataloguing-in-Publication Data A catalogue record for this book can be obtained from the British Library

Cover design John Good Holbrook Ltd, Coventry. Based on original drawings by Maryanne

Printing and binding Antony Rowe Ltd, Chippenham

Prison Patter

A Dictionary of Prison Words and Slang

CONTENTS

Acknowledgements

It would be quite impossible to list all the people who helped me to write *Prison Patter*, not least the hundreds of prisoners who replied to my request for examples of prison words and slang which was published in the prison newspaper *Inside Time*. Similarly, I have spoken to—and received contributions from—many other people, both prisoners and criminal justice practitioners with experience and knowledge of the special form of language which is the subject matter of this handbook. My appreciation extends to this entire 'army' of contributors, some of whom may well prefer to remain anonymous in any event!

There are several people to whom particular thanks are due. I am indebted to: Chris Tchaikovsky, Director of Women in Prison, for generously sparing time to check through the manuscript—and, among other items, for the Holloway version of the origin of the word *screw* (meaning *prison officer*) given on pp.11-12; to Phil Cooper, drugs educator and poet, for reading through the many drugs entries and offering his advice; to Nick Barnes at HM Prison Service Library for allowing me to study the internal Prison Service documents mentioned on page 19; to Mark Leech for the invaluable information contained in his work *The Prisoner's Handbook;* to Ann Morrell formerly of the Education Department at HMP Frankland; and to Bryan Gibson and Paul Cavadino for letting me summarise—in my introduction—parts of their book *Introduction to the Criminal Justice Process* when describing day-to-day prison life.

Omissions

Readers more familiar with prison regimes and prisoners than I am will doubtless be aware of words, expressions or nuances which I have missed—and may be able to improve on the contents of the present dictionary. If you know of items which have not been included, derivations of words and expressions, or think that an entry could be improved or updated, please send those details to me via Waterside Press, Winchester so that I can look at them with a view to their inclusion in subsequent editions.

Angela Devlin

November 1996

Necking

Prison Patter
A Dictionary of Prison Words and Slang

Introduction

BACKGROUND

This book came about through a sequence of coincidences.

Between 1992 and 1994 I interviewed prisoners in 12 prisons. I was researching for my book *Criminal Classes: Offenders at School* in which I tried to explore the links between educational underachievement and later offending behaviour. As a special needs teacher this was my first encounter with prisons, prison life and prison language. But I had taken a degree in English and have always been fascinated by words—particularly special language registers, those singular forms of communication peculiar to groups of people such as doctors, lawyers, journalists or schoolchildren. These language registers have often developed over a long period of time and their use is essential for people joining or wishing to progress or survive in a 'closed community'. Just for my own interest I began to note down prison words and expressions.

In the summer of 1992, my partner and I became the leaders of a campaign to correct what we believe to be a miscarriage of justice to Sheila Bowler, a local music teacher who was sentenced to life imprisonment for the murder of her husband's elderly aunt. As a novice in prison, her ear tended to pick out words and phrases that many other prisoners took for granted: during some of the lighter moments of our visits to her at HMPs Holloway and Bullwood Hall, and in our daily telephone conversations, she would often mention the strange or unfamiliar expressions used by other prisoners and by prison officers. At my instigation, she listened out for more to add to my collection.

Sheila Bowler also regularly sent me her copy of the prison newspaper *Inside Time,* and by 1995 I thought to ask that paper's readers for more examples. I received hundreds of replies. The editor had published just my initials—a lucky decision, as it meant that most correspondents assumed I was a man and their replies were quite uninhibited!

At about this point I compiled a short glossary for *Criminal Classes* and as I delivered this to the publishers, the editor, Bryan Gibson, read through it and then mentioned that for some time he had been toying with the idea of publishing a 'Dictionary of Prison Slang'—if only he could find somebody to write it. From that moment on we were in business! In less than six months I had collected some 2,500 examples of prison words, expressions, acronyms, jargon and officialese.

CONTENT AND METHODOLOGY

My starting point for including a word or expression was whether it occurred especially—even if not uniquely—in the world of the prison. Many of the entries in this handbook do occur only in prisons or in relation to prisoners, who adopt a special language register on arrival at an institution and discard it on release—much in the manner of children who may have one language for school and another at home. But many items in the book are used outside prison as well—because there is an inevitable overlap between words from the crime or drugs cultures, the criminal underworld and the world in general.

Slang words for criminals, certain crimes, the tools or proceeds of crime and aspects of the criminal justice process are commonly used inside and outside prison, as are certain other words, e.g. those for the police (**Bill, coppers, rozzers**) or male homosexuals (**bum bandit, faggot, poof**). But prisoners' conversations and letters were so peppered with them that I felt compelled to include them alongside some of the colourful, telling and often imaginative expressions generally used only on 'the inside'. In any event, prison language needs to be understood as a whole. My test for inclusion became whether words or expressions were part of prison language in its entirety—adding to the overall sense readers would gain about such places.

Various decisions needed to be made about the inclusion of what can broadly be described as 'impolite' words. My view is that it would have been wrong to sanitize the picture painted by prison language. There is still a 'macho' culture inside most men's prisons and neither these nor women's prisons are known for their delicacy. *Prison Patter* therefore sets out the language, warts and all: in adopting this approach I hope that no individual or group will be offended by the reality of the prison experience.

A good example of what I am describing occurs with those words used to vilify other people or groups of people. Some examples of names used by prison officers for prisoners (and vice versa) appear

10

under the heading *Jailers and the Jailed* later in this introduction. Perhaps understandably, some of the longest and often most derisory entries are for those held in particular opprobrium by prisoners. There are several uncomplimentary expressions in relation to the police from the overt **ACAB** (*all coppers are bastards*) to the subtlety of **lying squad** (formed via the simple expedient of docking the 'F' from Flying Squad) and the greater obviousness of **defective** (detective). The 25 words and expressions for the police listed in the handbook also include **filth** and **pigs**—although the majority of those entries are somewhat more 'user friendly'.

Almost as unpopular are informers (22 different words), and sex offenders (30). One of the longest entries is the group of 36 words for male homosexuals, reflecting the homophobia endemic in male establishments where the real or imagined fear of homosexual abuse is ever present. Again, it would have given an incomplete—indeed a misleading—picture if these words, even though unpalatable to anyone familiar with the duties cast by law on people involved in the administration of justice to avoid discrimination, had been removed. Prisons are not pleasant places and there is no point in pretending otherwise.

DERIVATIONS AND EXPLANATION

In compiling a dictionary of prison words and slang it is difficult to know how much explanation to include about a given item, the context in which it occurs, or its history. Thus, e.g. '**EDR** *earliest date of release*' provides the meaning of EDR but conveys little to the general reader. Similarly, a word like **reception** needs some explanation if only to enable readers to grasp the meaning of associated terms like **reception interview, Reception Board, reception letter** or **reception call.** All definitions must strike a balance between a version straightforward enough for lay people and absorbing enough for specialists—whilst a book of this kind can never hope to provide more than a rough guide. I hope I have achieved the correct balance.

Without claiming any definitive knowledge, I have included the derivations of words where I have been able to discover them. For instance I had always assumed the word **screw** to come from the turning of a key in a cell door but it has a much more interesting background. Women in nineteenth century Holloway were confined to their cells for silent working and on every cell door was a metal box full of small stones. The woman prisoner's job was to turn a handle inside the door which operated a mechanism to grind the stones into a

11

fine dust. A vindictive warder would screw the handle tighter with a spanner to make this work harder. The boxes remained on the doors of the old prison until it was demolished in the 1970s. Equally vivid is an alternative derivation which links the word to the ancient instrument of torture, the thumbscrew. In a recent **adjudication** at a men's prison, the governor reprimanded a prison officer who had put a prisoner **on report** for calling him a screw, which the officer regarded as a term of abuse. The governor overruled the adjudication on the ground that he considered the word to be derived from 'thumbscrew' and that its origin made it a valid historical expression!

Some prison expressions derive from slang used in HM Armed Forces, such as **AWOL** (absent without leave/missing)—reflecting the fact that officers or prisoners may well have served time elsewhere.

RHYMING SLANG AND BACKSLANG

Rhyming slang represents a language source all of its own. It is sometimes used to mask the truth, or to 'take the edge' off things, or to trivialise or undermine them. Examples are **bucket** (and *pail* = *jail*), **fillet** (of *veal* = *steel*) and **babbler** (*babbling brook* = *crook*).

Rhyming slang develops from what is usually a two or three word expression the last word of which rhymes with the true meaning. Then the rhyming part is dropped in favour of the non-rhyming and in itself meaningless part. It is thus ideally suited to the world of the prison (doubly so where drugs are concerned) in that it allows people to avoid reality and speak in code at one and the same time.

Certain words such as 'informer' words are particularly rich in rhyming slang. One of the most common, **grass,** may derive either from 'snake in the grass' or from 'grasshopper' = shopper' (*to shop* means 'to inform'). A simple term is **blade** (of grass); a more complex variant is **midnight mass.**

A further special type of derivation is backslang, in which a word, sometimes already a slang word itself, is reversed, for example **scran** out of **narc. Narc** derives from the Romany *nak* meaning *nose*—one of the many words for informer. A similarly interesting derivation, this time involving rhyming slang, is **Joe Gurr** (where *Gurr* = *stir*). Stir is one of a number of Romany words meaning *to confine*. The way in which slang develops can be seen in **whore's nark** (a loose reversal of Noah's Ark, itself rhyming slang for nark, which in turn is slang and has the probable origin already outlined). The mental dexterity demanded by this and other prison words indicates that there must be many people in our prisons who are neither **divs** nor **bagels**—or

12

balloons, cuckoos, Fraggles, headbangers or **mongs** (all common words for idiot in prison).

THE 'SECRET' DRUGS CODE

It was a hard decision whether to include the many words and phrases associated with drugs. My interviews with prisoners were peppered with these. Almost every communication I received contained several examples—perhaps inevitably as illegal drugs, criminal activity and the preoccupations of a certain proportion of the population are nowadays so drug oriented. As this book was going to press, a report published by the Penal Affairs Consortium vindicated my decision in favour of inclusion by pointing out that research findings show that 43 per cent of prisoners have used illegal drugs in the six months before imprisonment and that 11 per cent of male prisoners and 23 per cent of women prisoners are assessed as drug dependent. The report goes on to suggest that more than 5,000 prisoners may be drug dependent (*Drugs on the Inside,* Penal Affairs Consortium, 1996). However, one prisoner was highly suspicious:

> I have not listed all of the more secret words because for all I know you could be a policeman and—well, you know the bobby!

It would, in fact, be impossible to appreciate the language of the prison without knowing drug terms—many of which like **rhubarb and custard, pink champagne** or **Dennis the Menace** might easily pass for something else entirely.

Nothing dates faster than drugs slang. Its main purpose is to create a secret code designed to allow drug dealers and users to hide their activities and to conceal contraband from the authorities. If a term becomes too well-known it has to be changed. With a designer drug such as Ecstasy (see **E**) the list increases perpetually with the ever-changing colours, shapes or designs of the tablets. I decided to include substantial lists of drug words partly because of the frequency of these words in the prisons and partly because I am convinced that part of the fascination that the drug culture holds for young people is its secret language code, concealed from most adults—and yet so uncomfortably close to the world of crime.

The price of illegal drugs varies over time and from area to area: the estimates of prices quoted are valid as far as I can tell at the time of going to press.

13

JAILERS AND THE JAILED

Some words show the lighter side of prison life: in others its hidden brutality is revealed. Self-mutilation is common, depressingly so, especially in women's prisons: the routine use of words like **cutting-up, ligaturing, razoring, scratcher, slasher** and **slicer** gives only the faintest indication of the horror of these acts. Prison officers commonly refer to self-harm and suicide or attempted suicide as part of the **anniversary syndrome,** whereby prisoners are driven to despair on the anniversary of some emotional event such as the ending of a relationship or the loss of a loved one.

As with hospital jargon, prison officers' expressions may be clinical and serve to distance those in authority from the individuals in their care. Mechanistic phrases, initials and acronyms may be used—sometimes subconsciously—as a means of preserving power. Prisoners are routinely referred to as **bodies** or **numbers.** The use of surnames and prison numbers strips them of any status they might have enjoyed. The initials **DV** scribbled on a form give no hint of the trauma of domestic violence. After the birth of her baby a women may become a **BFM** (*breastfeeding mother*). An **emergency handout** is a baby separated from its mother in a prison **MBU** (*Mother and Baby Unit*) and handed over to a social services department outside (sometimes because the mother has breached prison rules). The term **lifer** is used in an almost dismissive way, giving no indication of the harsh reality of a life sentence. Since 1996, the written shorthand **life 4 life** has started to creep in, meaning life sentence prisoners who have been told that they will never be released. All these items have a depersonalising effect. Whilst researching the book, I was sometimes reminded of Jonathan Swift's nightmarish satire *A Modest Proposal* which uses analogous technical language in a plan for disposing of the Irish poor by butchering and cooking them. Indeed, officials throughout the criminal justice process commonly use the word **disposals** to refer to the cases (often meaning the people) passing through their hands.

Neither can the 'antiseptic' nature of much prison language be discounted. The crueller and more barbaric aspects of the prison experience may be concealed by euphemisms or black humour—whilst mundane and seemingly innocuous terms like **room** (*cell*), **segs** (*isolation, the punishment block*) and **harm** (*self-harm, self-mutilation*) mask reality.

Much prison language (that of officers as well as men in prison) is symptomatic of the macho 'nick culture' which still prevails in many prisons. Although the training of prison officers now places greater

14

emphasis on interpersonal skills, many officers continue to believe that 'a con is always a con' and the language they use to describe a prisoner ('manipulative', 'devious') can reflect contempt for their charges.

The same is true of prisoners' attitudes to prison officers. Mutual stereotyping is common. There are some 32 different terms for prison officers, from the humorously affectionate **kanga** (rhyming slang: *kangaroo = screw*) and the variants **Scoobie-doo** and **Dr. Who** via the mildly confrontational **German** (as if still the enemy over 50 years after World War II!) to the outright abuse of **shit-parcel**.

It is fascinating to compare the language sub-registers of the jailers and the jailed. A person remanded into custody for the first time is inevitably assailed by apprehension and fear, and the 'insider' language used by those already in the system is bound to reinforce this sense of strangeness and exclusion in the newcomer. It can be claimed that the use of unexplained jargon and officialese is a conscious strategy employed by those in power to assert their own superiority and exercise greater control by the deliberate withholding of information. It is certainly a wrong way of going about matters and encourages the kind of mind set that leaves prisoners open to other kinds of abuse.

Once they are part of the institution, however, prisoners seem quickly to assimilate the language of the jail: conversations with **LTIs** (*long term inmates*) can be just as mystifying to outsiders as those with prison officers because of the jargon they contain. By tapping into the language of power, showing an understanding of its complexities and using it effectively, prisoners reassert their own identity in an alien environment. However newcomers will also quickly pick up the *argot* of the prisoners' subculture and use that to achieve a sense of belonging and—eventually—to gain some kind of standing in their new peer group. England is a country where status is still defined to some extent by accent and the fluent use of language, and prison does no more than show this in microcosm. In jail there are of course many complex factors in the achievement of peer status, but one of them may be the acquisition of the specialist language which is the key to everyday social intercourse.

As part of another research project I was recently allowed to attend reception interviews on three consecutive days at a women's prison. Each prisoner is brought before the **Reception Board**—commonly consisting of a principal officer and another officer acting as an observer (in prison any such official interview is known as a **board**). It took only one minute for the interviewing officer to discover whether a woman had been in prison before: the language she used made it

15

immediately obvious. Once this had been established, an odd kind of camaraderie was set up between them, based on mutual understanding of a common language code. So a conversation might go something like this:

> *Officer:* Crown or Maj?
> *Prisoner:* Birmingham Crown—twelve and three—but I'm not sure if it's consec or concurrent. And there was me thinking I'd walk!
> *Officer:* Let's see—fifteen—consec I'm afraid. Ever breach bail?
> *Prisoner:* Yes, once. Missed going to the bill shop two days running.
> *Officer:* Got to be closed then. What's your domestic and your accommodation like?
> *Prisoner:* I'm on my tod—I'm NFA at the moment.
> *Officer:* Withdrawing?
> *Prisoner:* No
> *Officer:* OK. Well then—you're looking at twentieth March for your EDR.

(* See p. 20 for 'translation')

SCENES FROM PRISON LIFE

'Prison is rules, is rules, is rules!' said one prisoner I interviewed during my research. This perhaps understandable obsession with the regulations that govern prison life is reflected in many of the acronyms used by prison officials and the high proportion of officialese with a disciplinary connotation. A selection of the more common Prison Rules, conventionally referred to simply by number (e.g. **Rule 43**) is given in the Dictionary under **Rules.**

For readers unfamiliar with the prison system, it may be useful to give a short outline of the usual procedures whereby people come into jail, and an explanation of the average prison regime from reception to release.

From the court, a prisoner remanded into custody, or a newly convicted prisoner, will normally be taken, usually the same evening, to a local prison or remand centre. The new prisoner will be brought to the reception area, told to shower and given a meal, and may also be fingerprinted and photographed. He or she may then be issued with essentials such as washing things, a plate, mug and cutlery (all made of plastic), bed linen and clothing. Remand prisoners and women prisoners are permitted to wear their own clothes and extra clothing can be brought in by relatives the following day. Sentenced men usually have to wear a basic prison uniform. A few personal possessions like a wristwatch, radio, book and pen, may be retained at the governor's discretion—but all other property is held in a locker. A new prisoner is allowed a free **reception call** to relatives or friends (if he or she has any), and a free **reception letter.**

The following morning the prisoner will be given a medical interview to establish state of health (and sometimes pregnancy if a woman), suicide risk and fitness to work. Female prisoners and young offenders (under 21) have a simple allocation interview as most are categorized only as suitable for open or closed conditions. Adult male prisoners (over 21) are initially held in an **OCAU**—the observation, classification and allocation unit of a local prison or remand centre, and will then be given a security category from **Cat A** to **Cat D**. This will depend on the perceived risk of their escaping and the danger to the public should this occur.

Two special categories of prisoners may be segregated from others under **Rule 43** (Good Order and Discipline, or **GOAD**): prisoners who have committed sex offences or offences against children and are classed as vulnerable prisoners (**VPs**) needing protection; and prisoners who are considered a threat to GOAD and must be confined separately for the safety of others. Many men serving less than 18 months may serve their whole sentence in a local prison. Those serving longer will usually be transferred to a training prison. **Cat A** male prisoners will usually go to a high security closed training prison called a dispersal prison. **Cat A** women may go to a separate unit in Durham prison. Categorization is reviewed every 12 months and prisoners are usually moved to less secure conditions as they progress through their sentence.

Once a prisoner is settled in the allocated prison, a sentence plan should be drawn up for those serving more than 12 months and for all young offenders, aiming to ensure that time in custody is spent usefully and that attempts are made to tackle offending behaviour. Prisoners should be provided with work, training or education classes and be offered treatment programmes, although with overcrowding of prisons, increasing numbers of hours each day are spent locked in cells.

Prisoners are unlocked daily at about 8 a.m. and collect breakfast which they eat in their cells. Dinner is at 11.30 a.m. and tea—the final meal of the day—at about 4.30 p.m. Prisoners are entitled to a period of outdoor exercise daily, and to a set number of visits depending on whether they are convicted or still on remand, and whether they are on a **Basic, Standard** or **Enhanced** regime. These **differential regimes** were introduced in 1995 as part of a new national framework of incentives which includes six 'key earnable privileges', such as access to private cash, more community visits and longer time out of cell.

After tea, evening classes or **association** with other prisoners may be allowed, usually by rota, although, again, overcrowding and reduced staffing often means more prisoners locked up in cells. The regime of an open prison should of course be more relaxed, with prisoners freer to move around the prison and its grounds.

Some prisoners go on pre-release courses run by officers and outside agencies. Men serving sentences of six years or more, and women serving 18 months or more, may be allowed to spend the last six months of their sentence living in a **PRES** (Pre-release Employment Scheme) hostel either inside or outside the prison. They will seek regular paid work, contribute towards their keep and save for their release. A few prisoners may be considered for temporary release after they have served a specified part of their sentence. This enables them to take part in regime-related activities such as community service projects, employment, training or education. But these opportunities have been substantially reduced since the Home Secretary changed the rules for temporary release in 1994.

The Criminal Justice Act 1991 introduced new rules for the early release of prisoners and for their supervision and liabilities after release. Prisoners serving less than four years are released after serving half the sentence, unless 'additional days' have been added for offences against prison discipline—known as **ADAs**. Prisoners serving four years or more are released after serving two-thirds of their sentence (again subject to **ADAs**). If the sentence is between four and seven years they may be released on licence by the **Parole Board** between the half-way and two-thirds point. If the sentence is seven years or more, the Board can recommend release to the Home Secretary, who makes the final decision.

If a prisoner is serving a discretionary life sentence for an offence other than murder, the trial judge will set an appropriate tariff and the Home Secretary is required to release the prisoner after this tariff period if so directed by the Parole Board. If the prisoner has received a mandatory life sentence for murder, the Home Secretary sets the tariff and when it has expired may release the prisoner if the Parole Board recommends it. The Board has to be satisfied that there is no further danger to the public. Nevertheless, life sentence prisoners have to remain on licence for the rest of their lives and can be recalled to prison at any point. At the end of a sentence, prisoners are normally released after breakfast. Their property and clothes will be returned to them and they are given a discharge grant and if necessary a travel warrant.

GLOSSARIES AND LISTS OF PRISON WORDS

As far as I know, no other fully fledged dictionary of English prison words and slang has been produced. An American word list, *Prison Slang: words and expressions depicting life behind bars* was published by William K. Bentley and James M. Corbett in 1992 and prison *argot* has long been an area of study by sociologists interested in the prison environment, starting with Donald Clemmer's *The Prison Community* in 1940. It has also been used as a measure of 'prisonization', most notably by Ulla Bondeson in *Prisoners in Prison Societies* (1989) where she observes subcultures in Scandinavian prisons.

In England and Wales there have been at least three internal Prison Service documents. The first, a short *Glossary of terms and slang common in penal establishments*, was produced for Boards of Visitors in 1978. Ten years later, a second and more substantial document was produced by the Education Department at HMP Frankland, mainly for use by foreign national prisoners. The third document, *Welcome to the Prison Service* (Home Office, 1992) contained a glossary as part of a general introduction for new prison officers.

Other sources of comparable information are *A Dictionary of the Underworld* by Eric Partridge (first published in 1950) and Peter Quinn's entertaining piece *The Language of Prison* (*Justice of the Peace*, 149 JPN 218). Also, virtually as this book was going to press I learned of—and must acknowledge the benefit which I derived from—the short list of prison terms compiled by staff at HMP Hindley and contained in the *Prison Visits Training Pack* produced by the Magistrates' Association (1996).

MARYANNE'S ILLUSTRATIONS

One of the many prisoners I met during my first research project was Maryanne, a talented artist serving a short sentence for drugs offences. Her drawings have the irony and laconic wit of someone who has experienced all the vagaries of prison life at first hand. Now released, she lives in London with her young son.

PRISON PATTER

'I see you're interested in prison patter,' wrote one prisoner. There was my title! The letters from prisoners in response to my letter in *Inside Time* were full of prison wit and wisdom. The wry irony of prison life came through again and again in intriguing expressions like **ghosted** (*spirited away to another prison 'overnight'*), **green and friendly** (*prison phonecard*), **playtime** and **Wendy house** (*out of cells for association with other prisoners*), **plastic gangster** (*phoney tough guy*), **carpet** (*three months in prison is long enough to weave one!*), **on tour with the national** (*moving around the prison system courtesy of nation-wide travel arrangements*) and **shit and a shave** (*a very short sentence—also known as a* **bed and breakfast** *and a* **haircut**). Prisoners' farewell salutations were also in themselves fascinating in the way they reflected a survival culture and humour from adversity: **Keep your head down; Stay safe; Seeya round like a Polo; Take it Nelson!** (*nice'n easy*) and 'Wake up with a smile every day, the screws can't take that away'. One prisoner said he would close—after midnight—with these words:

I've got nish [nothing], no burn [tobacco], and I'm screwing [feeling hassled], so I'm passing a line two doors down [swinging a rope made of strips of bed sheet outside the window to the next cell but one] for a burn [tobacco] then I'm going to get into my crisp packet [bed].

Ultimately, for all its faults, it was the intriguing nature of prison language which kept me on track until I had accumulated the 2,500 or so words and expressions which appear in the Dictionary that follows. I hope readers will find it useful, educative and informative—and that it might in some small way assist better understanding of crime and punishment.

---

* Translation from p.16

Officer: Have you come from the Crown Court or a magistrates' court?
Prisoner: Birmingham Crown Court. I was given two sentences of twelve months and three months—but I'm not sure if they are to be served consecutively [one after the other] or concurrently [at the same time]. And there was me thinking I would be found not guilty and released!
Officer: Let's see [consulting the prisoner's papers]—fifteen months—that means your two sentences are to run consecutively I'm afraid. Have you ever breached the bail conditions imposed upon you?
Prisoner: Yes, once: I failed to report to the police station two days running.
Officer: That means you will have to be allocated to a closed prison. What is your domestic situation and what accommodation do you have?
Prisoner: I'm on my own and am of no fixed abode.
Officer: Are you withdrawing from a drugs habit?
Prisoner: No
Officer: OK. Well then, you're looking at twentieth March for your earliest date of release.

Prison Patter

A Dictionary of Prison Words and Slang

- Items in bold type also appear in the dictionary in their own right
- Those set out in capital letters are normally pronounced by the names of the letters, e.g. **ABH, TWC**
- Those set out in lower case are normally pronounced as written e.g. **ambov, twocking**
- A colon is used where the reader is being cross-referred to a 'key word' under which other common names are listed or general explanations given, e.g. '**pink champagne** *amphetamines (speed):* see **A**'
- A semi-colon is used where the reader is being cross-referred to comparable items, or items of similar interest, e.g. '**AAB** *assault and battery;* see **ABH, AOBH, PP nined**'
- All prices quoted for drugs depend on area, availability and season

A

A *amphetamines (speed)* a group of drugs often misused for their stimulant effect on the central nervous system. White or off-white powder or in pharmaceutically produced tablet form. Once commonly prescribed as a slimming drug. Usually sniffed or taken on the tongue, but can be dissolved in a drink or wrapped in a cigarette paper and swallowed. Cost £10-£15 per gram (1996). Other names include **benny, benz, billy, billywhizz, black and white minstrels, black bombers, dexies, energy powder, fast, fet, gofast, Lou Reed, olly, pink champagne, purple hearts, speed, sulph, uppers, white dust, whiz(z)**

AA *Alcoholics Anonymous* a fellowship of men and women who share their experience, strength and hope with each other in order that they may solve their common problem and help each other to recover from alcoholism

AAB *assault and battery;* see also **ABH, AOBH, PP nined**

AB *aggravated burglary* e.g. involving the use of a weapon, violence

ab *abscess* often from using drugs needles

ABE *Adult Basic Education* Basic literacy and numeracy classes are provided in prison

ABH *actual bodily harm* the offence of assault occasioning actual bodily harm contrary to section 47 Offences Against the Person Act 1861; see also **AAB, AOABH**

abscond (1) *escape;* see also **away, FTA, FTR, FTS.** (2) *quit bail*

ACAB *all coppers are bastards*

accumulated visits visiting orders (see **VO**) may be stored up and 'combined' if a prisoner is far from home. He or she is moved to a prison nearer to family and friends and allowed several visits packed into a short period

acid/acid tab *LSD:* see **LSD**. Also **acidhead, acid junkie, acid rapper** *LSD user;* see also **trip, triphead, tripper**

ACR *automatic conditional release* prisoners serving 12 months or more but less than four years are released at the half-way point of their sentence on licence (subject to conditions) and supervised until the three-quarters point of their sentence, known as the **licence expiry date** (**LED**). See also **AUR, DCR, parole, SED**

A D A *additional days added* punishment for breach of prison rules. The prisoner's release date is delayed unless he or she wins this **time back**; see also **ADR**

Adam, Adam and Eves *Ecstasy:* see **E**

Adidas *training instructor* after the Adidas logo which appears on sports equipment, including trainers and which mirrors the stripes on instructors' uniforms; see also **CIT, IO, SGO, two stripes**

admin *administration* i.e. the prison's administrative offices

ADT *Addictive Diseases Trust* now renamed: see **RAPT** *Rehabilitation for Addicted Prisoners Trust*

adjudication *disciplinary hearing* day-to-day process when **governor grades** deal with disciplinary matters; see also **nicked, nicking,**

on report, Prison Discipline Manual, telegram

A D R *additional days remitted* Additional days added (see **ADA**) can be won back, i.e. cancelled out for subsequent good behaviour; see also **time back**

advance new prisoners may be given an advance against their prison earnings to tide them over

advice prisoner term for a police reprimand, warning or caution

affray general description for a fight in a public place: 'I got done for affray' (not necessarily the offence of affray as defined by the Public Order Act 1986)

Afghan see **marijuana**

Accumulated Visits

22

AG *assistant governor*

ag/aggro *aggravation, trouble*

airhead after taking drugs

AKA *also known as* (police jargon): an alias; a false or assumed name

A-list prisoners in highest security category: see **Cat A** etc.

alkie, alky *alcoholic*

almonds *socks* (rhyming slang: *almond rocks = socks*); see also **mint rocks**

allocated/allocation to a particular prison according to offence, length of sentence, availability of accommodation etc; see also **temporary allocation**

Alphonse *pimp* (from rhyming slang: *Alphonse = ponce = pimp*)

Ambov/AMBOV *Association of Members of Boards of Visitors*; see also **BOV**

amp *ampoule* a small sealed glass container for drugs

amped *high on amphetamines:* see generally **A**

anger management controlling, managing anger, aggression etc. **anger management programme** course provided to help prisoners control such behaviour

animal *sex offender* other common names include:

> **bacon-bonce, beast, forty-three, monster, playing bingo, nonce, number, numbered off, on numbers, on the ones and twos, perve, Rule, Rule 43, scum, sex-case, VP, wrong 'un**

ankle straps *leather ankle restraints* used on prisoners considered to be violent; see also **bent up, C and R, closeting chain, shackles**

anniversary syndrome prison officer jargon for prisoners being more likely to self-harm or turn violent when an anniversary comes around e.g. a birthday of a loved one, or death in the family

AOABH longer version of **ABH**. Sometimes used loosely to describe assaults in general; see also **AAB**

Apex Trust charity that provides skills training and help for ex-prisoners

app *application* prisoners have to make an application to the governor for anything differing from normal day-to-day activities, e.g. anything brought in or sent out; a **transfer** to another prison; **accumulated visits**; to see the **chaplain, BOV** or a **probation** officer; sometimes called a **governor's** or a **governor's app**; see also **probation box.** Apps must be made to the **wing office** (generally in the morning)

appeal prisoners wishing to appeal must do so within set periods of time (different provisions apply to magistrates' courts and Crown Courts). A court may allow an appeal **out of time.** Also **appeal visit** special visit for lawyers to prepare an appeal; see also **legal visit**

apples/green apples *Ecstasy:* see **E**

APV *assisted prison visit* a grant may be available to help visitors with travel costs. APVs are only allowed to close relatives on income support or low incomes, who may get some or all of their costs paid by the Home Office. **APVU** *Assisted Prison Visits Unit*

A R D *automatic release date* prisoners serving sentences of less than four years are automatically released at the half-way point of their sentence unless there are additional days added (see **ADA**); see also **AUR, ACR**

area manager official with responsibility for a group of prisons within England and Wales

association time when prisoners are allowed out of their cells to meet, talk, play pool, watch TV, go to education classes etc. Association is regarded as a privilege. It can be withdrawn as a punishment, for security reasons or due to staff shortage. Prisoners not allowed association are locked in their cells; see also **free flow, full association, playtime, split association, Wendy house**

assisted visits see **APV**

attendance centre centre where offenders aged ten to 20 inclusive attend for 2-3 hours a week for a mixture of rigorous physical activity and instruction. Administered by the Home Office and usually run by police, often on Saturday afternoons. Attendance limits (up to a maximum of 36 hours) depend on age

attitude an attitude problem, a chip on the shoulder: 'That **screw's** got attitude!'

AU *assessment unit* where prisoners in prisons with therapeutic regimes are assessed

AUR *automatic unconditional release* prisoners serving less than 12 months are released 'unconditionally', i.e. not on licence, at the half-way point of their sentence. Although contained in statute, the term 'unconditional' is misleading because, on reoffending, the prisoner remains liable to serve the rest of the original sentence. This liability lasts until his or her sentence expiry date (see **SED**); see also **ACR, DCR, parole**

AV see **accumulated visits**

average roll average number of prisoners in a prison; see also **roll.** Compare **baseline, CNA, in use**

away a euphemism for (1) *in prison;* see also **in chokey, in jug, inside, in stir, in the nick, jugged.** (2) *escaped* as in **'one away!';** see also **cop a heel, legger, make one out, on the lam, on your toes, over the fence, over the hill, over the wall, trotter, walk, wallflower**

A W O L *absent without leave* (originally a military term); missing

B

B *Benzedrine:* also **benny, benz, black widow.** 'Benzedrine' is a tradename for amphetamine: see **A**

baby burglar *young thief*

babbler *crook* (rhyming slang: *babbling brook = crook*)

Babylon *police* (West Indian): see **Bill**

baccy *tobacco;* see also **burn, snout**

backdoor parole *dying in prison*

backhander *bribe;* see also **cop a drop, drink, grease/greasing palm, mump, on a pension, on the take, palm oil, soap**

bacon-bonce *sex offender* (rhyming slang *bacon bonce = nonce*): see **animal**

bad acid s e e **bad trip, LSD, flashback**

badge name badges are worn by some prison officers and this is Home Office policy. However, it was opposed by the **POA**. Some officers say they fear reprisals if prisoners know their names

bad rap *serious charge*

bad shit high quality drugs especially **marijuana**

bad trip taking **LSD** sometimes produces a feeling of panic, fear, dizziness or nausea; see also **DTs, flashback, horrors**

bag/bagel *standard measure of heroin;* see also **finger, joey, paper, sack, scorebag, wrap**

bagel, bagle *idiot;* see also **balloon, cuckoo, div, fraggle, fruitcake, headbanger, headcase, mong, muppet, nugget**

bagged *arrested:* see **nicked**

baghead *heroin addict;* see also **smackhead, smack freak, skaghead**

bagman someone in possession of drugs

bail a suspect may be granted bail (i.e. released) by the police to return to a police station, or, after being charged with a crime, by the police or a court for appearance at court. Conditions may be attached. **bail hostel** accommodation for people (assessed as suitable) whilst on bail. Often run by the local probation service. **bail office** a dedicated advice office

bait *credit* e.g. on drink, tobacco or drugs

balloon *idiot;* see **bagel**

B and E *breaking and entering*

bang *drug injection;* see **fix, hit, shot**

bang up (1) *inject drugs;* see also **dig, fire up, shoot.** (2) *lock in a cell;* see also **carpy, chubb up, dub up, lockup, miln up, shut down, total bangup**

barb/barbs *barbiturate(s)* a group of sedative drugs which suppress brain activity and can be misused; see also **goof balls, mandies, nembies, secs, tunes**

barbied *woman who has become subservient to a man* after the Barbie doll

Barney Rubble *Ecstasy:* see **E**

baron prisoner at the head of an extortion racket e.g. involving money, drugs or tobacco; see also **daddy, head**. Also used as a verb, as in baroning

Barts, Bart Simpsons, bartmans (after Bart Simpson the US TV character), **batmans** (after Batman, the US fictional crimefighter): see **LSD**

baseline baseline **CNA** *certified normal accommodation* the number of prisoners a prison can hold without overcrowding; see also **in use**

Basic *Basic regime* there are three levels of prison regime under the **differential regimes** system introduced in 1995, the others being **Standard** and **Enhanced**. The higher the regime, the more privileges e.g. with regard to **association**, visits, **private spends**. Basic regime is spartan and can be imposed for bad behaviour (offences against **GOAD**)

basil (sometimes **Basil Brush** after the glove puppet TV character (a fox) and *basil = weed = marijuana*: see **marijuana**

bastardize make one vehicle from two others (possibly involving disguise or fraud); see also **cut and shut**

Bastille mythical name used in connection with the riots at HMP Strangeways: sometimes nostalgically by prison officers: 'He was on duty at the Bastille'. Presumably by analogy with the 'storming of the Bastille' by members of a repressed French underclass

bath house communal showers and where clothing is exchanged: see also **kit change**

batphone *police radio* after the contraption used by Batman, the US fictional crimefighter

batty boy *homosexual:* see **bent**

beak *judge* or *magistrate*

beast (1)*child molester, sex offender:* see **animal** (2) *heroin;* see **H**

beat the rap withstand harsh interrogation

bed and breakfast *very short sentence:* see also **haircut, shit and a shave, weekend**

bed block/bed pack standard issue: sheets, blankets, cover, pillow cases and towels

bed watch supervisory duties if a prisoner is sick, at risk of self-harm or suicide, or a high security risk (inside or outside prison, e.g. in a hospital); see also **Pol I, special watch, SSS, suicide watch**

beggar's lagging sentence of 90 days: see **carpet**

behind the door locked in a cell/solitary cell; see also **banged up, lockup, shut down**

be like Dad *keep quiet* a play on 'keep Mum'

bender suspended sentence; see also **SS**

benny/bennies *Benzedrine tablet:* see **B**

bent (1) *homosexual* Other common names include:

batty boy, bum bandit, Burton, chutney ferret, clockwork orange, closet queen, cottager, cruiser, cupcake, fag, faggot, fare, fruit/fruitcake, gay, iron, iron hoof, nance, nancy, nancy boy, pansy, pillow biter, poof, poofter, puff, queen, queer, raver, screamer, shirtlifter, shit shover, turd burglar, wolf

(2) *corrupt* or open to bribery; **bent screw** *corrupt prison officer;* see also **safe screw.** Contrast **saint**

bent up method of restraint; see also **ankle straps, C and R, closeting chain, shackles**

benz *Benzedrine:* see **B**

BFM *breast-feeding mother* in a mother and baby units (see **MBU**)

bif, bifta (1) *cigarette;* see also **burn, civvies, oily, roll-up, salmon, smoke, strat, tab, tailor/taylor.** (2) enough **cannabis** (see **marijuana**) to make a **joint;** see also **bomber, draw, head, nightcap, puff, reefer, roach, roche, spliff, toke, zoot**

big A *AIDS*

big con *major confidence trick* Contrast **short con**

big H *heroin:* see **H**

big house *Crown Court* 'I was weighed off (sentenced) at the big house'

Bill *police.* Other common names include:

> **Babylon, bizzies, bluebottles, blue meanies, bobbies, bogey, bogies, bull, busies, coppers, cops, dibble, filth, flatfeet, fuzz, Mr. Busy, Mr. Plod, Old Bill, pigs, plod, reppocks, rozzers, Sweeney, the law.**

Also **Bill from the Hill** i.e. from Notting Hill

billet see **cell**

bills *underpants;* see also **skids**

bill shop police station; see also **copshop, factory, pigsty, plodshop, bussie station**

billy, billywhizz *amphetamines (speed)* in powder form: see **A.**

bird period in prison (rhyming slang: *birdlime = time*); see also **bit, cons, lagging, porridge, time.** Also **first bird** first prison sentence

birdeye *minute quantity of drugs*

birdman *prisoner;* see also **body, con, jailbird, lag, old lag**

biro *makeshift drugs needle* made from a Biro

bit *prison sentence;* see also **bird, cons, lagging, porridge, time.** **hard bit** *long prison sentence*

bit of work a *crime* especially a robbery

bizzies, busies *police;* see **Bill**

blab *inform:* see **grass**

black *blackmail*

black and white *police car;* see also **jam sandwich, panda, Q boat**

black and white minstrels *amphetamines* from black and white capsules and association with the 1960s TV variety show of that name: see **A**

black bombers *amphetamines (speed)* in tablet form: see **A**

black heart *depression;* see also **hump, get the**

Black Maria *transport for prisoners* A secure van with individual cubicles. Originally painted black. Other common names and descriptions include: **bus therapy, carrier, CV, meat wagon, paddy wagon, personnel carrier, sweatbox.** Contrast **transport, National Transport, on tour** with the **National**

black micro *microdots* of **LSD.** In tablet form

black pen *parole report;* see also **write up**

Black Prisoners' Support Group group set up in Manchester to offer help and support to black prisoners

black widow *Benzedrine:* see **B**

blade (1) *informer* from *blade of grass*: see **grass.** (2) *knife* generally meaning one made in prison. (3) *prison razor*

blag (1) *rob/snatch valuables* Thus **blagged** = robbed, **blagger/blag merchant** = armed robber; see also **taxing.** (2) *A confidence trick*

blank drugs mixed with non-narcotics: see **cut**

blank, to (1) *forget* e.g. childhood abuse. 'I just blanked it'; see also **check** (2) *ignore someone* (3) **get a blank** when e.g. parole is turned down; see also **KB, knockback**

blanket, on the to refuse to wear prison uniform. Often associated with IRA prisoners at the Maze Prison who regarded themselves as political prisoners and also conducted a **dirty protest**

blast *smoke drugs*

bleach tabs *sterilising tablets* sometimes issued to addicts to ensure drugs equipment is decontaminated

bleating *repeatedly denying guilt* (including by pursuing appeals). Convicted offenders - especially sex offenders - may seek to deny, distort or justify their behaviour, often to blame the victim.

blinker *police helicopter*

block *segregation unit* where prisoners who break prison rules are kept apart, or those at risk can be held for their own protection. The block usually consists of several cells, each with a bed, slopping out bucket, and a desk and chair all of which can be made of cardboard; see also **box, cage, cardboard city, CC, chokey, cooler, 1980 cell, protected room, rose garden, seg, sin bin, skid row, smokey, strip, strongbox, unfurnished room.** Also **put the block on** enforce rules strictly

blocker member of shoplifting team who distracts the store detective

blotters see **LSD**

blow (1) see **marijuana** (2) *inhale, sniff drugs*

blow your mind to have a hallucinogenic experience

blow out *collapse of case* usually meaning during a police investigation or during prosecution in court (sometimes called 'discontinuance'); see also **crash**

blow through *inform by telephone:* see generally **grass**

blue angel *Amytal* a barbiturate

bluebottles *police:* see **Bill**

bluefoot name used for white prisoners by black prisoners

blue meanies police: see **Bill**

blue papers official papers giving date of release; see also **AUR, ACR, DCR, parole**

blue stars see **LSD**

blues (1) *jeans* as worn by *convicted* prisoners; see also **browns, stripes.** (2) *convicted prisoners*

blue velvet drug based on antihistamine

bly *oxy-acetylene blowtorch* as used e.g. by a burglar

board *a prison panel* even two officers sitting in an office is enough to constitute a board. Examples are the **Reception Board** when new prisoners are interviewed; the Allocation Board when they are allocated to other prisons; the Labour Board (see **Labour 1, 2 and 3**) when prisoners are allocated work, education or training; the Transfer Board; the Sentence Planning Board; and the Home Leave Board

boarded up *protected from attack* especially from stabbing by other prisoners, often by inserting magazines under the clothing next to chest and stomach

bobby *policeman* (from Robert Peel, founder of the modern day police force, 1828): see **Bill**

Bobby Moore *knowing the score* (rhyming slang: after the captain of the England World Cup winning side of 1966 and for many years of West Ham United)

BOCDO *breach of conditional discharge order* i.e. of a licence condition following early release; see generally **ACR, DCR, parole.** Not to be confused with a court order conditionally discharging an offender at the point of sentence

Boarded up

body *prisoner* officers commonly refer to prisoners as 'bodies': 'Let's get those bodies moved from upstairs!'

body belt *body restraint* used in the **block** for prisoners considered violent; male belt has iron cuffs, female has leather cuffs; see also **C and R**

boffin *forensic expert*

bogart, to (1) *to overdose* i.e. on drugs. (2) to hold onto a **joint** to long (as in 'Don't bogart the smoke'). Presumably after the film actor Humphrey Bogart

bogey *police:* see **Bill**

bogwash hold someone's head down the WC and flush it

boiled mixture of sugar and boiling water made to throw at a prisoner or officer; see also **jugging**

bombed *stoned* on drugs

bomber *marijuana cigarette;* see generally **bif** and **marijuana.** Contrast a **black bomber** i.e. amphetamines (speed)

boney *genuine, OK, bona fide*

boo *prison:* see **clink**

Book, get the *to take to religion* whilst in prison; see also **glory, get the**

book, on the a prisoner considered to be a high security or other risk is put 'on the book'. His or her photo is placed a small book that must accompany him or her everywhere. In some high risk cases, officers log every movement and the prisoner is constantly accompanied (by up to four officers), even to the toilet; see also **closeting chain, E man, four to unlock, patches, stripes**

book, run a *run a gambling racket*

booked visit due to increased security some visits have to be booked in advance

booked *reprimanded* put on **report**

boot (1) bag of heroin; see also **paper, sack, wrap** (2) inhaling drugs from foil (rhyming slang *boot = toot = to inhale*). (3) use force, put the boot in

BOPO *breach of probation order*

BOSS *breach of suspended sentence of imprisonment* i.e. committing an offence during such an order

boss prison officer in charge e.g. laundry boss. Can also mean the prison governor; see also **bully beef, chief, screwdriver, white shirt**

Boss prisoners often call any male visitor or officer 'Boss' (and any woman 'Miss')

bottle *courage* **bottle out** *lose your nerve* e.g at the last minute before committing an offence

bottling *concealing in the anus* usually money or drugs, e.g. for transfer during a visit; see also **charger, chub, crutch, grease up, in the safe, plug, where the sun don't shine**

bounced out thrown off a prison drugs or alcohol treatment programme, e.g. for failing a urine test

bounty black prisoner's word for another black prisoner who seems to side with the 'white' authorities (derived from the 'Bounty' chocolate bar with 'black' chocolate outside and 'white' coconut inside; see also **coconut, sellout**

Bourne Trust national group which provides support for prisoners, ex-prisoners and their families

30

BOV *Board of Visitors* lay people appointed to act as a watchdog and look after the interests of prisoners. Each establishment has its own BOV. There are about 700 members of BOVs in England and Wales. Until 1992 they held adjudicatory and disciplinary powers. Prisoners are now disciplined by the governor, with the police brought in if an offence is felt to be sufficiently serious: see also **AMBOV**

box (1) *cubicle,secure arrangement* for one-to-one visit. (2) *punishment cell:* see **block**

boy *heroin* from connection between giving oneself a **bang** (i.e. a shot) and male homosexual intercourse; see **H**

boys in blue *security officers* in blue overalls who patrol the perimeter and may do **cell spins**; see also **burglar, squat team, swoop squad**

bracelets *handcuffs;* see also **cuffs, cross-cuffing, C and R**

brains/The Brains *detectives, CID;* see also **bull, defective, eye, lying squad, peeper, Sweeney, The Kremlin**

brassic out of money (rhyming slang: *boracic lint = skint*)

bratpan large, flat pan used in prison kitchens

bread *money* (rhyming slang: *bread and honey = money*); see also **Bugs Bunny, dosh, dough, lolly**

break *escape:* see **away**

breakfast prisoners sometimes refer to a sentence as 'Three months and a breakfast'. A prisoner is always offered a last breakfast on the day when he or she is released (normally at 8.45 a.m. or earlier). Superstition dictates that it should always be eaten, for luck and as a charm against returning to prison; see also **bed and breakfast, early riser**

brew, to *to heat up water and heroin* before injecting the mixture

brew *tea;* see also **(cup of) diesel, tea boat**. Also **brewed** *drunk*

brew pack *rations* usually issued at the rate of one per prisoner per week. Contain coffee, teabags, milk sachets and sugar

brick *cannabis:* see generally **marijuana**

brick it, to *to be really scared* (from **shitting bricks**)

bridge across a wing, between two side landings

brief (1) *lawyer* especially a barrister. From the file of papers, usually tied around with pink string, which is handed to a barrister by his or her instructing solicitor. (2) *search warrant*

bring down a disappointing or bad drugs experience; see also **bad trip, bummer, bum trip**

Brixton briefcase *portable radio/music centre;* see also **ghetto blaster, rad, rambler, sounds, talking handbag**

brown *heroin:* see **H**

brown bread *dead* (rhyming slang)

brown stuff *opium:* see **O**

31

brown tongue *informer:* see **grass**

browns (1) *jeans* worn by prisoners on remand; contrast **blues** (2) *remand prisoners*

bubble *informer* (rhyming slang *bubble and squeak = sneak/speak*): see **grass**

bucket *prison* (rhyming slang: *bucket and pail = jail*): see **clink**

bugging *telephone tapping* Calls by high security (**Cat A**) prisoners may be monitored and tape-recorded. Except in open prisons, any phone call can be intercepted and there may be random monitoring

Bugs Bunny *money* (rhyming sland, after the US cartoon rabbit): see **bread**

bull *detective:* see **brains**

bully beef *chief prison officer* (rhyming slang: *beef = chief*); see also **boss, chief, screwdriver, white shirt**

bum bandit *male homosexual:* see **bent**

bummer, bum trip *bad drugs experience;* see also **bad trip, bring down**

bumped told that another prisoner cannot pay a debt; see also **debthead**

bunco squad *fraud squad*

bung *a bribe* **to bung** *to bribe*

burglar *prison officer doing a surpise search:* see **cell spin.** Sometimes dressed in blue

overalls: see **boys in blue, squat team, swoop squad**

burn *tobacco cigarette;* see also **baccy, snout**

burn *deal in adulterated drugs*

burton *rent* (rhyming slang: *Burton-upon-Trent = rent*)

Burton(-upon-Trent) *homosexual* (rhyming slang *Trent = bent*)

bush see **marijuana;** see also **Kate Bush**

bussie station *police station:* see **bill shop**

bust, busted *caught, arrested* especially drug pushers/users

bus therapy *secure transport:* see **Black Maria**

busy, bizzy *policeman* especially a detective: see **Bill, brains**

butcher *prison dentist*

button *opium:* see **O**

buyer *receiver of stolen goods;* see also **fence, fixer, handling, placer**

buzz *effect of being high on drugs* especially from crack cocaine. **buzzing** *high on drugs* especially *Ecstasy:* see **E**

32

C

C *cocaine* a narcotic drug obtained from the leaves of *erythroxylon coca* and similar plant species indigenous to South America. May be misused for the feelings of euphoria and increased energy it produces. A white crystalline powder, costing £60 to £100 per gram (1996) and usually sold in half gram bags. Usually sniffed (see **snort**) but can be taken on the tongue, injected or smoked. Came to West in the late nineteenth century from Cochin China, from which the name, 'cocaine' comes. Other common names include

candy, cecil, charlie, coke, flake, girl, gonzo, lady, leaf, lemon barley, line, Mary Jane, nose (or nose candy), Patsy Cline, snow, stardust, stuff, white shit; see also **H & C**

For *crack cocaine:*see **crack**

C3 former division of the Home Office with responsibility for looking into cases of alleged miscarriages of justice. Now replaced by the Criminal Cases Review Commission, first proposed in 1993; see also **CCRC**

Cabbage Patch *HMP Kingston* (Portsmouth)

C A C *cubic air capacity* official amount of space allowed to each prisoner

CACS *centralised automatic control system* automatic computerised system for locking doors from a central control point; see also **control room, first unlock, numbers**

cage *confinement area* such as the block, a holding cell: see **block**

calendar *one year sentence;* see also **stretch**

Californians *Ecstasy:* see **E**

call signs as used by prison officers and police on their walkie-talkies. Based on the **NATO phonetic alphabet.** Meanings are same in any prison e.g.:

FOXTROT = farms and gardens; HOTEL = hospital; VICTOR = duty governor; ZULU = dog handler; X-Ray = vehicle escort; GOLF = gate; YANKEE = staff (e.g. canteen staff); WHISKEY = works; TANGO and PAPA = spare officers on patrol, each having a number so they can call each other: 'TANGO 1 to PAPA 2' etc.

can 1 oz of **marijuana**

candy *cocaine:* see **C**

candyman *drugs dealer*

cane *jemmy* for forcing doors, windows etc; see also **can opener**

CC (1) see **cardboard city.** (2) *cellular confinement* (usually in the **seg** *segregation unit* for breach of prison rules)

C and R *control and restraint* part of prison officers' basic training. Can mean (1) **riot gear** the body armour used by prison officers to deal with a dangerous prisoner. (2) *a secure room* where riot equipment is kept. (3) *an armlock* used to control a prisoner. (4) *restraints* e.g. handcuffs for men, leather wrist straps for women and a body belt if thought necessary; see also **ankle straps, bracelets, closeting chain, cuffs, shackles**

caning *taking drugs* especially **crack** cocaine

can opener *tool for breaking open a safe;* see also **jemmy**

canteen (1) *prison shop* The amount of money a prisoner can spend depends on whether he or she is on a **Basic, Standard** or **Enhanced** regime (see those items, **IEPS** and **private spends**). Prison canteens vary in what they provide (black prisoners sometimes criticise the lack of appropriate skin products). Cigarette lighters are usually on sale but must be of the see-through variety; **phone cards**, stamped with the words FOR USE IN HM PRISONS ONLY are sold, and books of stamps. (2) *food, cigarettes etc bought with money earned in prison.* (3) *to buy goods from the prison shop* (i.e. when used as a verb: 'to canteen'). (4) *place where prisoners' wages are paid out.* (5) *prisoners' earnings.* Also **canteen letters**: before the Woolf Report (1991) there was a restriction on the number of letters a prisoner could send out and stamps could be obtained in the canteen. Woolf proposed that prisoners can send out any number of letters. Prisoners all have one free letter a week and when they enter prison they get a free letter straightaway which is sent out by first class post. Many prisons are now imposing a ban on stamps being sent into prison because of fears that they can be impregnated with **LSD**

captured *arrested:* see **nicked**

cardboard city/CC (1) the **block** (where the furniture may be made of cardboard). (2) Also used as a verb **to be CCd** sent to the block (or this can simply mean to have a bed and table replaced by cardboard furniture)

care bear (1) *welfare worker* (2) *prisoners on a caring scheme* Seemingly, from the cartoon characters *The Care Bears.*

career a lifer's career plan; see also **sentence planning**

car key *screwdriver* for opening car doors

carpark *informer* (rhyming slang *car park = nark*): see **grass**

carpet *prison sentence of three months* long enough to weave a carpet; see also **beggar's lagging, double carpet** *six months,* **sorrowful tale, spell, three moon, tramp's lagging, tray** (probably from the French *trois*)

carpy, in locked in for the night (possibly from the Latin *carpe diem = seize the day*); see also **banged up, lock up, shut down**

carrier secure police van with cubicles; see generally **Black Maria**

carry a consignment/load of drugs

carry a case *to be released on bail*

carrying *in possession of drugs;* see also **holding** 'Are you carrying?' = 'Got any drugs?'

cart-napping *stealing supermarket trolleys*

carvie *prisoner who deals in contraband tobacco* a prison **baron** who carves up the tobacco

carzie WC; see also **kharzie, kazi**

case (1) *check out/weigh up a crime target* As in 'case the joint'. (2) *put on report* Also **caser** a strict prison officer: see generally **screw**

cash dispersal form to enable a prisoner's cash to be sent out of the prison

CAST *Creative and Supportive Trust* organization which helps women ex-prisoners acquire new skills and provides welfare advice and support

Cat A, B, C & D prisoners commonly refer to the prison they are in by its category (and see also **patches**). In fact it is the prisoners themselves who are categorized and allotted accordingly. Women and young offenders are categorized simply for open or closed conditions, apart from a few women who are categorized as 'Cat A'. This is reviewed every 12 months and prisoners tend to be moved to less secure conditions as they progress through their sentence. The current categories were defined in the Mountbatten Report (1966)

> **Cat A** Prisoners whose escape would be highly dangerous to the public, to the police or the security of the state, no matter how unlikely that escape might be; and for whom the aim must be to make escape impossible.
> **Cat B** Prisoners for whom the very highest conditions of security are not necessary but for whom escape must be made very difficult. Unsentenced prisoners are automatically categorized B unless provisionally placed in Category A
> **Cat C** Prisoners who cannot be trusted in open conditions but who do not have the ability or the resources and will to make a determined escape attempt.
> **Cat D** Prisoners who can be reasonably trusted to serve their sentence in open conditions

Cat A, to the categories are sometimes used as verbs e.g. 'They're going to Cat A me'

cat burglar climbs over rooftops, silently, usually in the dark; see also **dancer, high wall job, second storey man**

catweed see **marijuana**

CC two meanings may coincide (1) *cellular confinement* (usually meaning solitary confinement): see **block.** (2) *cardboard city*

CCRC *Criminal Cases Review Commission* the body proposed in 1991 to examine cases of alleged miscarriages of justice. In 1996 it took over these duties from **C3** division of the Home Office

cecil *cocaine:* see **C**

cell secure room; see also **billet, damper, drum, flowery, gaff, kennel, pad, peter, yard**

cell association a privilege enabling one prisoner to visit another in his or her cell, e.g. if two co-accused prisoners have decided to conduct their own defence and need to discuss strategy

cell spin *surprise search of a cell* often looking for drugs or weapons; see **room spin, spin, swoop, TO, twirled**

cell task pin-up (**task** = masturbation)

cement overcoat *buried in cement*

census office where incoming and outgoing mail is checked

centre (1) *middle of the prison* where the wings join up. (2) *prison officers' office*

centre punch used by burglars to make holes in window glass

CES *clothing exchange store* (i.e. in prison)

chaffy *fellow prisoner;* see also **mush**

change of appearance a prisoner is forbidden to change appearance (e.g. by dying hair, growing a beard). But an application (see **app**) can be made for permission to make limited changes

change of labour form a prisoner can apply for a change of prison job: see **Labour**

chaplain the official prison chaplain belongs to the Church of England, but all prisons have a Roman Catholic priest, a Methodist minister and/or leaders from other religions (e.g. an Imam) in their chaplaincy team; see also **sky pilot**

charge effect of soft drug use

charger *container* usually metal, bullet shaped. Used for anal retention of drugs etc.

charge room room in police station where people under arrest are charged and searched

charge sheet (1) on which alleged offence(s) against prison discipline are listed; see also **Rules, the** (2) handed to an accused person when bailed by police. Sets out the allegation

charlie *cocaine:* see **C**

chase, chase it, chase the dragon burn heroin on foil and inhale it through straw, moving quickly from left to right: see generally **H**

check/check out *blot out of the mind;* see also **blank**

chief/chief officer *senior prison officer;* see also **boss, bully beef, screwdriver, whiteshirt**

chiffy *prison weapon* made from razorblade attached to a toothbrush handle; see also **piece of steel, shiv, striper**

chillout room *recovery room at a rave* set aside for dancers who have been **buzzing** on, e.g. *Ecstasy* (see **E**). Other drugs are often sold unlawfully to assist this: see **tems**

children's visits some prisons set aside special days when prisoners' children can spend time with their parents. Carers/other relatives leave children at the **gate** and they are escorted by an officer (often in civilian dress) to meet their parent. These are sometimes **full day visits** from about 9.30 a.m. to 3.30 p.m. Children up to age 16 are allowed to visit, say, once a month. Activities and refreshments may be provided; see also **HALOW**

chin *to punch on the chin*

Chinese *heroin cut with white powder* (i.e. adulterated): see generally **H**

choirboy *new police officer;* see also **rookie**

choke off *tell off/punish a prisoner* (prison officer slang)

chokey (1) the **block** (possible from Hindi *chauki = a shed*). (2) time spent on the **block**

chop the clock reduce the miles shown on a vehicle's mileometer; see also **clock/clocking**

chore *steal* 'He chored that food from the kitchens.'

chubbing *anal smuggling* bringing items into prison by conceaing them in the anus; see also **bottling, crutching, greasing up, in the safe, plugging, waxing up, where the sun don't shine**

chubb up *lock a cell door* from the Chubb brand name; see also **bang up, dub up, miln up**

chucks (1) *withdrawal* from drug addiction or other habit. (2) *excess, overeating, vomiting*

chutney ferret *male homosexual:* see **bent**

CIT *civilian instructor/trainer:* see also **Adidas, IO**

CITC *Construction Industry Training Course*

civvies (1) *cigarettes* bought rather than hand-rolled; see also **bif/bifta.** (2) *plain clothes* as worn by **governor grades**. In certain open prisons, some officers have elected to wear civilian clothing where appropriate e.g. the female officer in charge of an **MBU**

civvy *civilian* an instructor or visitor not in uniform; see also **suit**

clap *gonorrhoea* (from the old French *clapoir = a sore caused by venereal disease*)

claret *blood* especially drug use: 'There was claret all over the fit' (blood all over the syringe)

Class A, B, C drugs. Under the Misuse of Drugs Act 1971, controlled drugs are divided into classes A, B and C

Cell Spin

clattered *beaten up*

clean (1) *unarmed* (2) *drug-free* having succeeded in beating addiction; see also **straight**

clean up *make a killing* get away with a big profit

cleaners, take to the *rob, strip, swindle*

clink *prison* Other common names include **boo, bucket, dolls' house, fillet, Joe Gurr, jug, nick, slammer, stir**

37

clip joint *nightclub set up to fleece customers*

clipper (1) *cigarette lighter* After those originally sold under the 'Clipper' brand name. Matches are not always allowed in prison. Small, transparent, disposable lighters may be bought from the canteen for about 80p (1996); see also **scratcher** (2) *woman who robs punters under the guise of selling them sex;* see also **roller**

clock, to (1) *size someone up.* 'When I was a new officer on the wing I could sense the inmates clocking me!' (2) *wind back the mileometer on a vehicle* as in 'clocking cars'

clocked when an illegal activity has been observed; see also **sus**

clockwork orange *homosexual:* see **bent**

cloddy *prison officer:* see **screw**

closed visit a visit supervised by prison officers when the visitor is separated from the prisoner by a screen. With increasing concern about contraband (especially drugs) being smuggled into prisons, more closed visit boxes are being constructed. Communication is via a meshed screen. A prisoner can be 'put on closed visits' for a period of 14 days if under suspicion of smuggling drugs, or for 28 days or more if there is actual proof of this; see also **crutching, downing, necking**

closet queen *male homosexual who keeps sexual preferences secret;* see **bent**

closeting chain a *restraint* carried by officers escorting a prisoner.

Enables the prisoner to use the toilet/provide a urine sample etc. in privacy while ensuring security. Consists of handcuffs on a long chain which remains attached to the officer and can be passed under a toilet door; see also **ankle straps, C and R, cuffs, shackles**

clucking *craving for drugs* especially **crack** cocaine (see **C**) as in 'I was clucking for crack'.

clue up *provide information* , e.g. to new prisoner; see also **give someone the office, SP**

C N A *certified normal accommodation;* see also **baseline, CNA, in-use**

coat 'slag off"

cob *prison food* especially bread; see also **cobitis, duff/duffer, whodunnit, yelow peril**

cobbler *forger*

cobblers *rubbish* (derived from rhyming slang: *cobblers' awls = balls*)

cobitis *aversion to prison food;* see also **muck truck, slop time**

cockle *ten years in prison* 'a ten stretch' (rhyming slang: *cockle and hen = ten*)

coconut see **bounty, sell-out**

co-D *co-defendant*

coke *cocaine:* see **C** Also **coke head, coke freak** *cocaine addict;* see also **snow bird**

cold turkey *all of a sudden coming off drugs/alcohol;* see also **turkeying**

collared *arrested;* see also **nicked**

combination order *community sentence* which combines one to three years' probation with 40 to 100 hours' community service

combo *combination lock*

come clean *confess* especially a crime to the police; see also **cough, sneeze out**

come down effect when drugs wear off

commie *computer*

community visit modern name for a **town visit** whereby a prisoner can go out to visit a place near the prison in the company of relatives or friends. Only applies to open prisons, some young offenders and female prisoners assessed as suitable. The right is also part of the 'Incentives and Earned Privileges Scheme' (see **IEPS**). Prisoners can be out for six hours a day, usually from 9.30 a.m. to 3.30 p.m. They can go anywhere (with any number of family or friends if they wish), but usually within a 20 mile radius of the prison

compact *'contract' between a prisoner and an instructor, officer, governor.* Can be a simple compact when a prisoner agrees, for instance, to join a work party, abide by the rules and work. Or it can be used when someone has broken prison rules. Both parties sign a document whereby the prisoner promises to be of good behaviour in return for privileges; see **incentives, IEPS**

compassionate *compassionate licence* modern name for 'compassionate leave' which is granted to certain prisoners (see also **temporary licence**). Only granted in exceptional, personal circumstances, e.g. to see a dying relative; attend a funeral; for child care hearings where a prisoner is the primary carer; for marriage or some religious ceremony; to attend medical appointments. Normally limited to five days in every month.

compassionate release in a rare case the release of a prisoner can be ordered on compassionate grounds, e.g. terminal illness, tragic family circumstances

complaint see **R and C**

con (1) *prisoner;* see also **birdman, body, jailbird, lag, old lag.** (2) *confidence trick;* see also **big con**

con artist/conman *confidence trickster;* see also **grifter**

concerted indiscipline serious incident in breach of prison rule

concurrent two or more sentences to be served at the same time, e.g. six months and six months concurrent = six months in total; contrast **consecutive**

confidential access a prisoner who feels a request or complaint has not been adequately dealt with by prison staff can write a request or 'complaint' in a sealed envelope to the prison governor, chair of the Board of Visitors (see **B O V**), or Prison Service Area Manager. See **R and C, reserved subjects, PCU, Prisons Ombudsman**

cons *sentence;* see also **bit, bird, lagging, porridge, time**

consecutive sentences to be served one after the other, e.g. six months and six months consecutive

= 12 months in total: contrast **concurrent**

containered *locked in a cell*

contracted prisons the official name for privatised prisons (sometimes called 'contracted out'). There are some differences in terminology between state-run and private prisons but the Prison Rules apply to both. Private prisons have a **Director** rather than a **Governor** and prison officers are called **Prisoner Custody Officers (PCOs)**; see also **privatisation**

control room *centre of operations* the nerve centre. CCTV screens show each area of the **perimeter** and of the prison. Officers check in here each morning to collect their walkie talkies. Where tannoy announcements are made from, e.g. orders for unlocking; see also **CACS, first unlock, numbers**

convictitis *fear of prisoners*

cooking *preparing drugs*

cooler see **block**

cop a drop *accept a bribe:* see **backhander**

cop a heel *escape:* see **away**

cop a plea *plead guilty* perhaps to a lesser charge under a deal

cop out on *inform on:* see grass

cop/copper (1) *policeman:* see Bill. Also **copper jitters** *extreme fear of police* (2) *large prison kitchen cooking pot* **copperman** *prisoner in charge of the* **'coppers'** in the kitchens

coppers' nark *informer:* see **grass**

cop shop *police station;* see **bill shop**

cornering *a form of fraud* selling stolen goods to tradesmen, then retrieving them by posing as police officers

corporation cocktail *coalgas bubbled through milk*

cottage *public urinal* **cottager** *male homosexual* who picks up partners in public lavatories; see also **cruiser**. Also **cottaging** picking up homosexual partners in public lavatories: see **bent**

cough *confess;* see also **come clean, sneeze out**

couriering *smuggling* (usually meaning drugs through customs); see also **finger, mule**

cow and calf *50 pence* (rhyming slang: *cow and calf = half [a pound]*)

CPC *Certificate of Professional Competence* gained on prison courses

CPN *community psychiatric nurse* some prisons, especially open prisons, have an arrangement to call upon a local CPN when needed

CPS *Crown Prosecution Service*

crack *crack cocaine* made by steaming acetone, water and raw cocaine in a glass tube or bottle so it cracks up into crystals referred to as **rocks**: see generally **C**. Crack produces a more rapid and intense reaction than cocaine, which wears off quickly. Each 'rock' costs £15 to £25 (1996) and is smoked in pipes or cans or from **foil**; see also **stone, wash**. Also **crackhead** crack-cocaine user; **crack house** where crack dealers operate

crapper dick plainclothes police who try to catch homosexuals in public lavatories

crash when police drop a case; see also **blow out**

C R D *conditional release date* prisoners with a sentence of between 12 months and four years are released automatically at the half way point in their sentences unless any additional days (**ADAs**) have been imposed for breach of prison rules: as in **ACR**

creamer person stealing from the till when working in a shop or business; see also **inside job**

creeper burglar who operates while owners are in the house; see also **on the creep**

crisp packet *prison bed* 'because that's what it feels like when you get into it!'

CRO *Criminal Records Office* sometimes used as a verb: 'The police CROd me.' (I.e. checked my record)

cross-cuffing the use of handcuffs where a prisoner's left hand is attached to the escorting officer's left hand for extra security. Also known as **left hand to left hand**; see also **bracelets, cuffs, C and R, shackles**

cross-sex posting employment of men officers in women's prisons and vice versa (since 1986)

crotch walker shoplifter who conceals stolen goods between thighs

crown *Ecstasy:* see **E**

'Crown or maj?' Question commonly asked of a new prisoner by the officer at the reception interview to find out if the sentence of imprisonment came from the Crown Court or the magistrates' court

cruise *search the streets for a male homosexual partner* Used as a noun (i.e. **cruiser**) to describe people who do this; see also **cottager**

crutching smuggling contraband goods especially drugs by hiding them in a condom and inserting them into the vagina (often followed by a tampon). Prison officers can carry out a strip search but not an internal examination (which requires special authorisation). In response, some prisons have experimented with **closed visits,** whereby suspects are segregated from visitors in closed boxes with partitions; see also **closed visit, downing, necking**

CS (1) *community service* (2) *custody sergeant* the designated police officer responsible under **PACE** for prisoners in the police station

C S L A *community sports leader award*

CSO *community service order*

CSP *Cognitive Skills Programme* therapeutic course to teach prisoners about the likely consequences of their actions

CSV *Community Service Volunteers* organization which arranges full-time volunteer placements in the community for young people and has some imaginative projects placing young offenders in full-time community service

cube *morphine:* see **M**

cuckoo mentally disadvantaged; see also **bagel, bagle, balloon, div, fraggle, fruit/fruitcake, headbanger, head case, mong, muppet, nugget**

c u f f s , c u f f e d *handcuffs, handcuffed;* see also **bracelets, closeting chain, cross-cuffing, C and R.** Also used as a verb: **to cuff** to handcuff

cupcake *male homosexual;* see also **bent**

cup of diesel see **diesel**

cushy nick a prison with easy going regime, good facilities

custody days if a prisoner is held in custody on **remand** this time will ultimately be taken off his or her sentence; see **remand remission**

Cup of Diesel

custody for life while life imprisonment is the mandatory sentence for murder committed by a person aged 21 or over, in the case of an offender age 18 to 21 when the murder was committed, the equivalent mandatory sentence is called 'custody for life'. Until the offender is over 21 he or she can be kept in a young offender institution. If convicted from age 10 to 17 inclusive, the equivalent is known as detention at **Her Majesty's pleasure**

custody officer (1) police custody officer responsible for ensuring compliance with **PACE** at a police station. **(2)** *prison officer in a private prison;* see also **c o n t r a c t e d prisons, PCO**

cut (1) *dilute/mix drugs* with other drugs or substances; see also **blank (2)** *stab*

cut and shut car made from the front of one vehicle and the back of another; see also **bastardize**

cutchie receptacle for smoking drugs (West Indian origin)

cut up *self mutilate* usually by slashing forearms with a razor or broken glass; see **razoring, scratcher, slasher, slicer;** also **cutter** self-mutilator

cut-throat *prison razor*

cut up touches *brag about crimes committed in the past*

CV *cellular vehicle* prison transport with individual cells for dangerous or high security prisoners: see **Black Maria**

D

dabbling *illicit dealing,* usually meaning in antiques or drugs; can also mean homosexual activity

dabs *fingerprints;* see also **wild prints**

daddy leader/strong prisoner/top dog/head of racket; see also **baron, head**

dark day *night duty* prison officer jargon; see also **detail**

damper see **cell**

dancer *cat burglar;* see also **high wall job, second storey man**

D and D *drunk and disorderly*

Danny Marr *car* (rhyming slang)

DC *detention centre* (1) holding centre for illegal, or allegedly illegal immigrants; see also **deportee, detainee.** (2) former institution for young offenders (often associated with one-time Home Secretary, Lord Whitelaw) to provide a 'short sharp shock'. Now replaced by young offender institution (see **YOI**); see also **detainee**

DCR *discretionary conditional release* prisoners serving four years plus can be released following a recommendation from the Parole Board at any time from the half-way point of their sentence, staying under supervision until the three quarters point; see also **AUR, ACR, parole**

DDU *drug dependency unit*

deal (1) *any sort of trade* prisoners must rely only on small amounts from prison earnings or **private spends,** so that for much of the time they 'trade' instead. Trades are known as **deals. Phonecards** are a common currency. Other prison currency includes stamps, **brew packs,** Mars bars, cigarettes and tobacco; see also **dimps, private spends.** (2) *drugs deal* or a deal involving other contraband items

Dear John letter a letter bringing bad news, usually ending a relationship; used outside prison, but the phrase has a particularly poignant significance for someone who is incarcerated; see also **Johnny letter**

debthead prisoner continually in debt, not to be trusted; see also **bumped**

debts *placed on report* 'I got my debts for calling that **kanga** a bastard!'

deck, decker *measure of drugs*

Decree 33 Nigerian Government decree making drug couriers imprisoned outside Nigeria liable to further imprisonment when they return home (thus creating double jeopardy in breach of international principles of justice)

defective *detective:* see **brains**

Dennis the Menace *Ecstasy:* see **E.** From the comic book character and the red and black stripes on some tablets which match Dennis's sweater

dep *deputy prison governor* officer responsible for the prison in the **governing governor's** absence

deportee foreign national who is liable to be deported. Can be (1) a

43

convicted prisoner who has been recommended for deportation. (2) an illegal, or allegedly illegal immigrant, many of whom are held in **detention centres;** see also **detainee**

d e p s *depositions* copies or transcripts of evidence given by witnesses and victims. Prisoners may study these with a view to an appeal. Some insist on fellow prisoners reading their deps to scotch rumours that they are guilty of child molestation or sex offences; see also **nature of charge, Rule 43**

designer drugs *imitative drugs* such as Ecstasy (see **E**) which copy the effects of more expensive pharmaceutically produced drugs. Many unlawful drugs can now be classed as 'designer drugs' in that they are produced at home. Often use pure ingredients (i.e. other drugs neat) and can thus be extremely dangerous to people accustomed to diluted drugs or drugs **cut** with other, non-narcotic substances

detached duty when prison officers go to another prison for a period. If a jail is short-staffed, or needs more male or female staff, it will 'borrow' officers. Staff volunteer and may get improved remuneration to compensate for temporary disruption; see also **vols**

detail prison officer's turn of duty; see also **dark day, detached duty, vols**

detainee (1) foreign national who is liable to be deported; see also **DC** (2) young offender detained in a custodial institution; see **also YOI** (3) a suspect detained by the police under **PACE**

detention/detention centre see **DC, detainee**

detox *detoxification centre, service, or programme* Also used in the sense 'in detox', i.e. when, or after, giving up drugs

dexies *Dexedrine* amphetamines (speed) (*dextroamphetamine*) in tablet form: see **A.** Central nervous system stimulant, once prescribed as a slimming drug

DFs *DF118* brand name for a drug which is often misused for its narcotic effect

dibble *police:* see **Bill**

Dickless Tracy *female police officer* (from US fictional detective Dick Tracy)

diesel *cup of prison tea;* see also **brew, tea boat**

differential regimes a nation-wide framework of incentives and privileges was introduced in 1995. Prisoners are placed on one of three regime levels: **Basic, Standard** or **Enhanced.** According to the regime, they are given various privileges. There are various 'key earnable privileges': **private spends; visits; community visits;** enhanced earning schemes; time out of cell; permission to wear own clothes (male prisoners only; all female prisoners wear their own clothes); see also **compact, IEPS, incentives**

dig *inject heroin* (or other drug); see also **bang, fire up, fix, hit, shoot up, shot, shoot.** Also used as a noun i.e. 'a bang', 'a shot'

dimps *small amounts of money* (or other jail currency, e.g. tobacco); see **deals, private spends**

dipper/dipping *pick pocket;* see also **diver, fingers, nudger, whizz, whizz mob, the whizz**

dip squad *police who target pickpockets*

director *'governor' of a private prison;* see also **contracted prison**

direct order where a direct order is given it is an offence against **GOAD** to refuse to obey. Failure to comply can lead to an **adjudication**

Director General head of the entire Prison Service

dirty dishes *false evidence;* see also **frame-up**

dirty protest *smearing excrement, pouring urine around;* see also **on the blanket, pissed cell fashion, potting up, shit shaped**

dis *disrespect* wrong someone

discharge *release* prisoners are normally released after breakfast. Their property and clothes are returned and fresh clothes supplied if necessary; see also **liberty clothing**

discharge grant grant to cover expenses until a released prisoner can claim benefit/find work. The amount depends on age and whether the prisoner will be homeless. The equivalent of one week's income support and one week's payment of any extra benefit for which the prisoner qualifies. Not a gift, but an advance against payment of future benefits to tide the prisoner over. Later deducted

from any benefits which are due. A **travel warrant** is usually issued as well; see also **gate money**

discharge hygiene pack *pack of condoms and lubricants* issued free of charge to prisoners on release/temporary release

discipline officer *prison officer:* see **screw**

disclaimer form on **reception** into prison, a prisoner has to sign a disclaimer which accompanies a property card (**prop card**). This states that he or she accepts responsibility for any possessions he or she decides to retain. There is a limit on what can be kept. Other property must be listed on the prop card and kept in a secure property box (**prop box**); see also **swagged off, two box system, volumetrics**

disco biscuits/disco burgers *Ecstasy:* see **E**

disclosure meeting *therapy meeting* where a group of prisoners describe their offences or, e.g. recall abuse, offences

discretionary life sentence life sentence for an offence other than murder, e.g. manslaughter, attempted murder, rape, arson, armed robbery, kidnapping, causing an explosion. The **tariff** is fixed by the trial judge and at the end of this period the decision whether to release the prisoner is made by a **Discretionary Lifer Panel (DLP)** of the **Parole Board,** consisting of a High Court Judge, a psychiatrist or probation officer and a lay person. Some lawyers specialise in representing Discretionary Lifers at their **DLPT** (Discretionary Lifer Panel Tribunal). All lifers are released on a **life-licence** which remains in force for the rest of their lives and which can be revoked at any time and the person recalled to prison; see also **custody for life. mandatory life sentence, Her Majesty's pleasure**

DLP *Discretionary Lifer Panel* a panel of the **Parole Board** which sits to consider the case of a prisoner on a discretionary life sentence: see **DCR**

dish out the gravy *sentence harshly*

dispersal prison *high security closed training prison* an institution capable of holding high risk prisoners. Male **Cat A** prisoners are dispersed among maximum security dispersal prisons (hence 'in dispersal'): see **Cat A**

disposal processing offenders through the criminal justice system. Also used to refer to prisoners e.g. 'We had six disposals from the Crown Court this morning'; see also **bodies**

div, divvy *stupid person* (possibly from divot meaning clod of earth, or the Romany *divio* , mad). Also a weak prisoner; see also **bagel, bagel**

diver *pickpocket;* see also **dipper, whizz, whizz mob, the whizz**

DLPT *Discretionary Lifer Panel Tribunal;* see **discretionary life sentence**

DMO *drug-misusing offender*

do a bit *serve time in prison;* see also **do time**

do for *kill*

do over *assault*

do time *serve time in prison;* see also **do a bit**

dock asthma when the accused gasps with surprise at accusations in court

dock brief tradition whereby any accused person in the dock could legitimately demand that any barrister present in court represent him or her on payment of half-a-crown (22.5p). The barrister had to be wearing robes. Nowadays superseded in practice due to legal aid

dodgy *informer;* see **grass**

dog-ender prisoner who collects cigarette-ends to re-roll into new cigarettes; see also **swooper**

dog tag *prescription* often for drugs, possibly forged, unlawful; see also **hit the doctor, script**

doing books *stealing* or *forging benefit books,* e.g. child benefit

doing cards *stealing* or *forging credit cards;* see also **on the plastic, photogenic**

doing time *serving time in prison;* see also **do a bit**

dollar *Ecstasy:* see **E**

dolls' house *prison:* see **clink.** Contrast **Wendy house** = **association**

dolly *morphine:* see **M**

dolly bag *cloth bag carried by women prisoners*

done *beaten up;* see also **sorted**

46

done up *assaulted;* see also **do over**

dolphin *Ecstasy:* see **E**

dope see **marijuana**

dose (1) *four month sentence* (2) *venereal disease* (3) *medication*

dosh *money* combination of do(llar and ca)sh; see also **bread, Bugs Bunny, dough, lolly**

dosser (1) *someone who sleeps rough* 'on the streets'. (2) *layabout, lazy person*

double back, double bubble *interest* demanded by e.g. drug/tobacco barons who lend out and get double back; see also **two for one**

double carpet *six month sentence* (a **carpet** = three months)

double cherry drops *Ecstasy:* see **E**

double dooring *hotel bilking* non-payment of bills

dough *money;* see also **bread, Bugs Bunny, dough, lolly**

doves *Ecstasy:* see **E**

downer (1) *barbiturate, sedative, tranquilizer* (2) *legal medication* abused by drug takers to help them 'come down' after taking illicit drugs, Valium, Librium, Mogadon, Temazepam; see also **barbs, jellies, tems, tranx, vallies.** (3) *depressing event* (4) *addict* prisoner addicted to pills; see also **pill-popper, speed freak.** Also **downing** swallowing illicit drugs, to be retrieved later by excretion; see also **necking**

down time free morning or afternoon when prisoners working part-time can visit the **canteen**, etc

DPA *Deprived Prisoners' Aid* this charity provided clothing and other help to destitute prisoners. Since the mid-1960s it has been superseded by the through-care of the **probation** service, **NACRO** and other organizations

drag back where a prisoner has been released on licence (see **AUR, ACR, DCR, life licence**) he or she can still be 'dragged back' to prison if there is a breach of licence or other legal ground

dragon *heroin:* see **H.** See also **chase**

draw *cannabis cigarette* enough for a single **joint:** see also **bif, bifta.** See generally **marijuana**

dread (1) *frightening* 'It's dread, in the Old Bailey.' (2) name used by white prisoners for black prisoners (probably from 'dreadlocks')

drink *bribe:* see **backhander**

drop (1) *take drugs* by swallowing. Also **drops** ill-gotten gains stashed away (2) see **LSD.** Also **drop tabs** to take **LSD;** see also **blotters**

drop in centre (1) somewhere prisoners can discuss problems in confidence. (2) *educational resource centre*

drug-free zone/wing area housing prisoners who reject drugs; see also **VTU**

drum see **cell**

47

drum *dwelling-house* 'I was robbing rich people's big drums'; see also **spin a drum**

drummer *confidence trickster* usually posing as a door-to-door salesman; see also **knocker**

Dr Who prison officer (rhyming slang = *screw*. From the eponymous character in the long-running BBC TV series): see **screw**

dry bath *strip search;* see also **strip**

drying out *withdrawing* coming off alcohol or drugs

DTs *delirium tremens* 'the shakes', withdrawal symptoms often signifying that the person concerned craves alcohol after a brief period without it

dub up *lock a cell door;* see also **bang up, behind the door, chubb up, miln up**

duds *fake drugs*

due likely to get arrested

duff, duffer *jail pudding;* see also **cob, cobitis, whodunnit, yellow peril**

dukes *fists* (possibly from rhyming slang *Duke of Yorks = forks = fingers*)

duty dog a **governor grade** who is on duty when the **governing governor** is away, or after hours; may be the **dep** *deputy governor*

DV *domestic violence*

dyke (1) *lesbian* (2) *dipipanone* a narcotic analgesic drug often misused for its euphoric effect

E

E *Ecstasy* (MDMA). A controlled drug, a hallucinogenic amphetamine which stimulates the central nervous system. Taken orally. Costs £10-£15 per tablet or capsule (1996). Other common names include:

Adam, Adam and Eves, apples, Barney Rubble, black and whites, Californians, crown, Dennis the Menace, disco biscuits, disco burgers, dollar, dolphin, double cherry drops, doves, echoes, fantasia, Gary Abletts, green apples, happy, heaven sent, hug drug, lemon and limes, love doves, love hearts, mints, New Yorkers, om, omega, pills, pink cadillac, pit bulls, power pills, red hots, rhubarb and custard, saucers, scorpions, snowballs, snowhearts, tablets, tangerine dreams, tangoes, Thatchers, triple-Xs, white burgers, white doves, Xs, X-Files

Names often come from designs, colours or shapes of tablets; see also **designer drugs**

early riser prisoner about to be discharged, an event which usually happens in the early morning, straight after breakfast; see also **breakfast, discharge**

earn *make money by unlawful, possibly criminal means* **earning** making money, usually unlawfully, especially buying and selling drugs **earner, nice little earner, real earner** (1) *easy money* usually unlawful (2) *a good result* in court or in response to a request whilst in prison (see **C and R, app**); see also **result, squeeze**

ears see **listeners**

earwig *lookout man;* see also **hogman**

easy! *hello!*

echoes *Ecstasy:* see **E**

ECV *earned community visit* a **community visit** is the modern name for a **town visit**

ED *evening duties* prison officer term

Edna! *Watch out, keep quiet, get out!* (rhyming slang: *Edna May = on your way*). Edna May was a well-known music hall artiste

EDR *earliest date of release* old term, but still often used to describe a prisoner's automatic release date (see **AUR, ACR, ARD**) or eligibility date for parole (see **DCR, EDP, PED**)

EFC *Employment Focus Course* to improve skills and help prisoners find work on release

eggs *temazepam* used improperly: see **tems**; see also **downers** (contrast **uppers**), **green eggs, jellies, tranx, wobbly oggs**

eighth eighth of an ounce of a drug; see **marijuana**

elephant *heroin:* see **H**

eleven-fifty a prisoner's police or prison file

E-list *escape list* prisoners felt to be a high security risk are put on this list. **E-man** prisoner who has made an escape attempt or is under suspicion of trying to escape: see **away**

EMC *effective minimum complement* the number of staff required to run a prison safely

EMD extended main duty when an officer's normal duties are extended

emergency handout handing out of a prisoner's baby from an **MBU** to the care of local aurhority social services. Usually happens when the baby is nine to 18 months old or the mother has breached prison rules. It is unlawful for a baby or child to be locked into a prison cell; see also **handing out**

EN *enrolled nurse*

energy powder *amphetamines (speed):* see **A**

Enhanced regime highest of the three regimes under which a prisoner can be held. It affords extra privileges such as more **visits,** more **private spends.** The other regimes are **Basic** and **Standard:** see **differential regimes**

enhanced visits *extra visits* e.g. an extra visit every other month (see also **VO, PVO**)

enrol *join* a prison class or course

EP *existing prison* where prisoner is currently held

EPD *earliest parole date* under the modern early release scheme, prisoners serving four years or more are subject to discretionary conditional release (**DCR**). EPD signifies the earliest date at which discretionary release can happen. Another term used is 'parole eligibility date' (see **PED**). Strictly speaking, parole as such has ceased to exist but the term is still

49

commonly used to describe discretionary conditional release; see also **parole**

equipped (1) going about equipped with a weapon. (2) contrast the criminal offence of 'going equipped' contrary to the Theft Act 1968, i.e. for any burglary, theft or cheat

'er indoors wife/female partner (in modern times associated with the fictional character Arthur Daley and the ITV series *Minder*)

ERP *Early Release of Prisoners* in 1992, a fresh scheme for early release was introduced. Prisoners serving less than four years are released unconditionally after serving half their sentences (unless additional days are added: see **ADA**); see also **AUR**. Prisoners serving 12 months but less than four years are released on licence at the half-way point but subject to conditions (and subject to **ADA**); see also **ACR**. Prisoners serving four years or more are released after serving two-thirds of their sentence (again possibly with **ADA**); see also **DCR**. They may be released on licence between the half-way (see **EPD, PED**) and two-thirds point (see **NPD**) of their sentence. The **Parole Board** deals itself with DCR in relation to prisoners serving between four and seven years; but if the prisoner is serving seven years or more, it can recommend release to the Home Secretary, who makes the decision. Certain release provisions are under review (1996)

escape committee prisoners planning (or fantasising about) an escape; see also **wallflower**

escort, on escort *prisoner escort* officers detailed to accompany prisoners on journeys outside the prison, e.g. to court, another prison or hospital; see also **external duties**

ESL *English As a Second Language* prison education department course.

establishment *prison* officialese

estate the entire body of prisons in England and Wales (i.e. the 'prison estate'). It is often sub-classified as the **female estate** or the **male estate**

ETA *expected time of arrival* prison officer jargon: 'What's the ETA of the Holloway escort?'

EV *extended visit* all prisons have discretion to allow the length of certain visits to be extended

ex-con *ex-prisoner* short for 'ex-convict'

exercise daily period of fresh air in the 'exercise yard' to which prisoners in closed prisons are entitled. In open prisons there are no fixed exercise periods. Juveniles and young offenders serving short sentences should have physical exercise every weekday

external duties any prison officer duties outside the prison, including being **on escort**

eye *detective:* see **brains**

eye! eye! *warning* that a prisoner is under surveillance; see also **nitto! on top!**

F

F75 report report on a prisoner serving a life sentence. Carried out periodically and compiled by the lifer's **personal officer**, probation officer, wing officer and lifer **liaison officer**, with input from other people connected with the prisoner, e.g. the education staff, a psychologist etc. The F75 affects moves and the prisoner's security category

face notorious or 'high-ranking' criminal, well-known to police and the underworld

facility licence a form of **temporary licence;** prisoners eligible to apply are fixed sentence **Cat C** and **Cat D** prisoners who have completed at least a quarter of their sentences; such a licence can be granted for regime-related activities, e.g. community service, employment, training and education courses, or for official purposes. e.g. going to court, seeing legal advisers. Must not be recreational nor attract public concern

factory *police station:* see **bill shop**

fag, faggot *male homosexual* (derived from US slang): see **bent**

fall arrest; see also **nicked.** Also **to get a fall** to be arrested. **fall guy** someone set up to be arrested, a scapegoat; see also **patsy**

fall money money kept aside to pay lawyers if a suspect is arrested

fantasia *Ecstasy:* see **E**

fare *client* of (1) *woman prostitute* (2) *male homosexual prostitute;* see generally **bent**

fast/go fast *amphetamines (speed):* see **A**

fell off the back of a lorry euphemism for stolen goods

female estate see **estate**

fence *receiver of stolen goods;* see also **buyer, handling, placer, receiver**

fet *amphetamines (speed):* see **A**

fillet prison (rhyming slang: *fillet of veal = steel (bars)*); see **clink**

filth *police:* see **Bill**

finger (1) **put the finger on** *inform* on someone, point them out to the police; see also **grass, hot up** (2) *little finger of a surgical glove* used as a packet for drugs imported by swallowing; see also **courier, mule**

fingers *pickpocket* traditional; see also **dipper, diver, nudger, whizz. whizzer**

First Bird

51

fire up *inject drugs*; see also **bang, shoot**

firm (1) *gang* (usuallly criminal, and inside or outside prison). **firm-handed** to belong to a gang. (2) prisoners who bully/intimidate other prisoners on the instructions of people who believe themselves wronged

first bird *first prison sentence*

first unlock when prisoners are let out of their cells in the morning; see also **CACS, control room, numbers**

fish *new prisoner;* see also **new fish, star**

fishbowl the visits room at Wormwood Scrubs. Prisoners say it is like being in a goldfish bowl; see also **goldfishing**

fit *outfit* drugs equipment; see also **gear, kit, works**

fit for work the prison doctor decides whether or not prisoners are fit for work and they are then put into the categories **Labour 1, 2** or **3**. Sometimes used as a verb: 'to fit for work'

fit up *give false evidence*; see also **fix, flaking, frame, frame up, jobber**

five finger money derived from shoplifting; see also **hoisting**

fives *fifth landing* in a prison

fix (1) *provide false evidence* usually with the object of implicating ('fixing') someone. (2) *inject drugs;* see also **bang, dig, fire up, hit, shot** (also used as nouns)

fixer agent in the pay of the police; see generally **grass**

flake *cocaine:* see **C**

flaking *planting evidence* maybe implying an allegation that this has been done by a corrupt police officer

flash roll of low value banknotes with a high value note wrapped around the outside, to give an illusion of affluence, wealth

flashback a return to the experience of a previous **trip** during drug taking, months or even years ago, often due to **bad acid** (see **LSD**); see also **bad trip, horrors**

flatfeet *police:* see **Bill**

flatworker burglar specialising in flats

flea powder *heroin* **cut** with other, similar looking substances: see generally **H**

Flintstones, flints see **LSD**. From the cartoon characters *The Flintstones*

flop *safe house*

flowery *cell* (rhyming slang: *flowery dell = cell*); see also **cell**

flue *prison officer* (rhyming slang *flue = screw*); see **screw**

fly a kite *pass a forged cheque;* see also **kiter, lay a kite, leafer, paperhanger**

flying *high on drugs*

flying pasty *bag of excrement* thrown from cell window (more common before sanitation installed in cells); see also **line, swing, swinger**

Flying Squad *top police detectives* usually meaning **Scotland Yard,** but sometimes nowadays applied to Regional Crime Squads (proposed to become a 'National Crime Squad': 1996); see also **bull, eye, defective. lying squad, peeper, Sweeney**

FNF *Friday night fracas* prison officer jargon for prisoners on a charge relating to a Friday fight mêlée, often after drinking when wages have been paid out

FOCUS *Financial Outstation Central Unified System* Prison Service accounting system

foiling (1) *making fake coins* out of special foil for use in slot machines. (2) *deactivating security devices* usually meaning on garments in chain stores by using metal foil

Follies, the *Quarter Sessions* old term. These courts were abolished and replaced by the Crown Courts under the Courts Act 1971

form/former *criminal record* former convictions: 'Has he got form?', 'Any former?'; see also **mileage, pc, previous, record, sheet, yellow sheet**

food boat when several prisoners club together to pay for food; see also **tea boat**

Forty three prisoner on **Rule 43** for safety of self or others. Also used as a verb: 'He was forty-threed'; see also **animal**

four be two prison officer (rhyming slang = *screw*) and may come from army slang, where it means a piece

of rag, four inches by two inches, used to clean guns, or from do-it-yourself, where it means a plank of wood four inches wide by two inches thick; see also **screw**

four to unlock the strict regime imposed on a potentially dangerous/violent prisoner. It means four officers being present when, e.g. the prisoner's cell is unlocked and this label will commonly be transposed, e.g. four to feed, four to wash etc. Similarly, two or three to unlock

Fours the fourth landing in a prison; see also **Ones, Twos, Threes, Fives**

four stretch *four years in jail* (a **stretch** is a year)

FP *false pretences* old description for some fraud offences involving money, property

FPFSG *Federation of Prisoners' Families Support Groups* Umbrella organization for groups giving help and support to prisoners' families

FPWP *Female Prisoners Welfare Project* which supports women in prison and helps them to keep up links with their families; see also its sister group **Hibiscus**

fraggle (1) *mentally ill prisoner* prisoner usage (from the American children's TV programme *Fraggle Rock*); see also **bagel, bagle, balloon, cuckoo, div, fruit, fruitcake, head banger, head case, mong, muppet, nugget.** Also **fraggle juice:** medication given to mentally ill prisoners; **Fraggle Rock:** psychiatric wing, landing or psychiatric criminal care unit (**PCCU**): compare **funny farm,**

Muppet house (2) *insulting name for prisoners considered stupid*

frame *incriminate innocent people;* see also **fix, fit up, flaking, frame.** Contrast **in the frame.** Also **frame-up** *false means of getting an innocent person convicted;* see also **jobbed**

freak out (1) *bad drugs trip;* see also **flashback** (2) *get angry, violent*

freebase *free the base* take all impurities out of a drug so that its effect is heightened and more immediate

free flow movement, usually lightly escorted, of prisoners from wings to education, canteen or chapel or to various occupations

Fresh Start the 1987 initiative developed after a dispute between the Home Office and the Prison Officers' Association (**POA**), which restructured working practices; see also **TOIL, unified grades**

frisk (1) *body search* (usually meaning by the police); see also **pat down, rub down** (2) *have a laugh*

front it (1) leave a **VPU** (Vulnerable Prisoners' Unit) and go back into the main prison. (2) face up to a given problem; see also **strong it**

front man *spokesperson* or *leader* of an illegal activity/organization, appointed (and usually paid) to give it respectability; see also **laundromat**

front money money paid in advance for drugs (derived from US slang)

fruit, fruitcake *male homosexual* (derived from US slang): see **bent.** Also **fruitcake** *mentally ill prisoner;* see also **bagel, bagle, cuckoo, fraggle, mong, muppet, nugget**

FT *full term* of a sentence

FTA *fail to arrive* e.g. at court; see also **abscond, FTS**

FTE *full time education*

FTR *fail to return* to prison, e.g. after home leave

FTS *fail to surrender* to custody; see also **abscond, FTA**

fuck-off merchant an officer who always fobs prisoners off; see generally **screw**

full association when prisoners are allowed out of cells for the whole of the scheduled period in the evening, e.g. from returning from work at 4 p.m. until 8 p.m.; see also **association, free flow, split association, playtime, Wendy house**

full day visit some prisons arrange 'full day visits' for children from about 9.30 a.m. to 3.30 p.m. Children up to the age of 16 are usually eligible; see also **children's visits**

full sheet complaint by prisoner against a prison officer

funky yellows see **LSD**

funny farm mental hospital; compare **Fraggle Rock**

funny money *forged money*

funny papers see **LSD**

fuzz *the police:* sco **Bill**

G

G5/grade 5 see **governor grades, unified grades**

GA *Gamblers Anonymous* nationwide organization for people wishing to forsake gambling

Gabriel a prisoner who plays the organ in the prison chapel

gaff see **cell**

gag a bit of fun, excitement: a **buzz**

gallery *rogues' gallery* police book of photographs of potential suspects; see also **mug shot**

game, on the game *prostitution;* see also **going case, hooker, hustler, turning tricks**

ganja/gunja generally **marijuana**

Gary Abletts *Ecstasy* (rhyming slang *Abletts = tablets*); see **E**

gat *hand gun* a pistol or revolver (from US: short for Gatling gun); see also **heater, rod, shooter**

gate *main entrance to a prison* where all visitors must report with **ID** on arrival, and sign out on departure. At the gate, officers and other prison staff collect their keys at the start of their shifts by surrendering a numbered metal disc and hand back their keys at the end of the day. There is a buzz of activity at the gate each morning at about 7.45 am when the morning shift arrives. Remand prisons are especially busy at this time when the huge prison gates are opened for secure transport vans to enter and collect prisoners for court or other prisons: see **Black Maria, transport, National Transport.** At most other times at closed prisons the main gate remains closed. Entry is via a small door within or beside it. Even in open prisons there is a 'gate house' and usually a barrier to prevent vehicles driving straight into the prison. Increasingly, open prisons are installing secure gates and fences, especially female establishments (less to prevent absconders perhaps than to deter intruders). Also **gate arrest** when a prisoner has completed his or her sentence but is rearrested immediately on leaving the prison and charged with other offences or detained as liable to deportation; see **detainee.** If the police have informed the prison that this is their intention, the prison governor is obliged to let the prisoner know. But there is no corresponding obligation on the part of the police to inform the governor, so that many prisoners remain anxious about release; **gate fever/gate happy** exuberant, excited, moody or anxious about forthcoming release; **gate money** amount given to prisoners on release; see also **discharge grant**; **gate pass** permission to leave the prison granted to prisoners on **temporary release** or who are allowed to work outside the prison

Gate Lodge official magazine of the **POA**

gauching state after taking drugs, i.e. glazed eyes, open mouth

gavolt a 'mini-riot'

GBH (1) *grievous bodily harm* usually meaning the offence of causing grievous bodily harm contrary to section 18 Offences

Against the Person Act 1861 (i.e with intent). It may mean the lesser offence of 'malicious wounding' contrary to section 20 of the 1861 Act (which does not require the same level of intention or *mens rea*). Both offences involve serious injury to the victim, though short of death (when an offence based on the same events would usually become one of murder or manslaughter). (2) the drug gamma hydroxy butyrate (actually **GHB**, but 'GBH' is commonly used instead). Used for body building and as an aphrodisiac; see also **hardcore, liquid e, liquid x.** Also **GBH of the eardrums** *loud music;* **GBH of the brain** *studying*

Mileme   Ghosted.

gear (1) *drugs* often heroin (see **H**)). (2) *drugs equipment,* e.g. syringes; see also **fit, kit. outfit, works**

gee *inform:* see **grass**

Geese/Geese Theatre theatre company working inside prisons and across the criminal justice process. Actors (all professionals) use drama therapy and other techniques to confront denial, distortion and other defence mechanisms used by offenders to explain away their crimes, thereby allowing prisoners to face up to issues affecting their offending behaviour. A central technique is that of 'the mask' whereby actors and prisoners adopt two persona: one presenting a front to the outside world (masked), the other revealing true inner thoughts and feelings (unmasked). Outside prison the Geese often make presentations of their work which rely on performance, audience participation and spontaneous interchanges about crime and offending. A 1996 review in *The Magistrate* described the Geese Theatre as a 'unique contribution to criminal justice'

German see **screw**. As if still the enemy these 50 years after World War II. Mainly Liverpool area/Scouse usage

get bladdered *get drunk*

get the book *to be reprimanded*

get the Book *become religious* Book = Bible; see also **get the Glory**

get your shit together *get organized* as in 'Get your act together!'

GHB (1) *gamma hydroxy butyrate* commonly called **GHB** instead. Used for body building and as an aphrodisiac, es[ecially in gay use;

56

see also **hardcore, liquid e, liquid x.** (2) *Ecstasy:* see **E**

ghetto blaster *portable music system;* see also **Brixton briefcase, rad, rambler, talking handbag**

ghostbusters see **LSD** From the fictional characters in the 1980s film and song

ghosted *spirited away* to another prison, usually overnight or early in the morning with very little, if any, warning. Property is usually left to follow. A prisoner might not have time to warn visitors; see also **on the ghost train, sent to ghost town, shanghaied, shipped out, skulldragged**

girl *cocaine* so called because it is meant to be a female aphrodisiac: see **C, lady**

girls *women prisoners* usually referred to by officers (and sometimes by each other) as 'girls', whatever their age

Giro *benefits cheque* **to do giros** to get someone else to sign a giro cheque and cash it, then for the intended recipient to go to the post office and report it as lost

give (someone) the office *initiate someone* especially a new prisoner; see also **clue up, SP**

glass, glass up, glassing to cut someone's face with a broken glass or bottle (amounting to the offence of **GBH**)

glasshouse detention cells, punishment block (from military punishment block)

glory, to get the to take to religion in prison, see also **Book, get the**

glue, doing glue sniffing solvents; see also **nosebag, spray, stickup**

GO *gym officer or orderly:* see and compare also **Adidas, PEI, PEIO, PEO**

go away *go to prison;* see also **away**

gobgrabbing trying to grab drugs thought to be concealed in another prisoner's (or a visitor's) mouth. i.e. gob; see also **downing, necking**

GOAD or **GOD** *good order and discipline* which is dealt with by the Prison **Rules**

go down *go to prison* sometimes literally meaning down the court steps

go fast *amphetamines (speed):* see **A**

going case *prostitution;* see also **game, hooker, hustler, turning tricks**

go into one get into a violent rage

gofast *amphetamines (speed).* see **A**

gold, gold seal see **marijuana**

gold dust *heroin:* see **H**

goldfishing term used to describe behaviour by visitors when being shown around a prison; see also **fishbowl**

GOM *God's Own Medicine* morphine: see **M**

57

gone *under the influence* of drugs, alcohol, music, religion etc.

gonzo *cocaine:* see **C**

good lad prisoner trusted by fellow prisoners

good stuff *high quality drugs*

good time *remission of part of sentence* nowadays meaning the part of a sentence served in the community under the early release provisions; see also **AUR, ACR, DCR, parole;** or may mean **time back**

goods *critical evidence* 'He's got the goods on me!'

goof balls *barbiturates:* see **barb/barbs**

go out poncing *search for men working as pimps,* i.e. by the police

go over the fence, go over the hill *escape:* see **away**

go sick *see the prison doctor* ; see also **vet**

go Queen's *turn Queen's evidence* i.e. give evidence against co-defendants (usually in return for improved treatment by the authorities)

goulash *meat stew* of any kind in prison

gov *prison governor;* see also **love, light of, old man**

governing governor the most senior governor at a particular prison

governor grades there are eight **unified grades** in the Prison Service. Thus e.g. a **Cat A** high security prison would be likely to have a governor 1 in charge, while a governor 3 might be in charge of an open prison. An **area manager** will also belong to the highest grades. Below the **governing governor** at any establishment, the hierarchy is a deputy governor (see **dep**) and then a number of assistant governors. There is some overlap between governor grades and the more senior prison officers, who are either chief officers, principal officers or senior officers. A basic grade prison officer will occupy grade 8

governor's adjudication a governor's on a disciplinary matter, or ruling on a **governor's app**

governor's app *application, request to a governor for permission;* see also **app, complaint, R and C form**

grab (1) *arrest* **grabbed** *arrested:* see **nicked.** (2) prison wages

graft *go out and commit crimes* as if working

grand *£1000* (derived from US, $1000)

grass (1) see **marijuana.** (2) **grass, grasser** an informer. **to grass** to inform, to **rat on,** to **shop** (rhyming slang: *grasshopper = shopper,* also *grass in the park = nark*); see also **blab, blab through, squeal.** Other common names include:

> **blade, brown tongue, bubble, carpark, dodgy, fixer, gee, midnight mass, nark, noah's ark, nose, scran, snake, snide, snitch, snout, squealer, Ssss . . .**

stoolie, supergrass, whore's nark

gravy *prison sentence* **dish out gravy** = to sentence harshly

grease/greasing palm *bribe:* see **backhander**

grease up put vaseline round the anus in order to smuggle contraband inside it, e.g. drugs and money; see also **bottling, charger**

green and friendly *prison phone card:* see **phonecard, phonecard deal**

green apples *Ecstasy:* see **E**

green eggs *temazepam* can be sold in the form of green or yellow egg shaped capsules: see **tems.** Also called **eggs, jellies and wobbly eggs**

green form form used to apply for preliminary or emergency legal aid (the term having been extended in prison so as to apply to applications for legal aid in general)

green micro, green penguins see **LSD**

grievance *official complaint by a prisoner* by writing to the prison governor. If the complaint is more serious, it can go to the **area manager**; see also **app, governor's app, R and C form**

grifter *confidence trickster;* see also **con artist**

GRIP *Gay Rights in Prison* organization to advise and support bisexual, gay and lesbian prisoners

grooming stealthily building up the confidence of a planned sex victim (often a child)

Group Four *private sector organization* concentrates on secure prisoner **escort** and **transport** services

groyne *ring* (in jewellery theft)

Grupo Amiga organization which helps Spanish/Portuguese speaking women, usually from Latin America, in British prisons

guardian angels prisoners trained to assist others in matters of bullying etc.

GUC/GUM *genito urinary clinic/medical* unit for the treatment of sexually transmitted diseases

gunja/ganja see **marijuana**

gutted *very upset;* see also **roasting, screwing**

H

H *heroin* a synthetic narcotic morphine-derived drug which depresses the central norvous system, comes in fine powder form (off-white or brown). Costs £60-£100 per gram. Usually sold in £10-£20 **wraps** (1996). Smoked (chasing the **dragon:** see **chase**), dissolved or injected. Other common names include **beast, big H, boy, brown, chinese, elephant, flea powder, gear, gold dust, Harry, Henry, horse, junk, scag, skag, shit, smack, stuff, quill, tackle, the nasty**

habit *serious addiction to drugs;* see also **hurting, jones, monkey**

H and C *taking heroin and cocaine together* as in mixing hot and cold water; see also **C, H, speedballing**

haircut *short sentence;* see also **bed and breakfast, shit and a shave, weekend**

half a stretch *six months sentence* (a **stretch** = one year)

half a ton £50 (a ton = £100)

half inch *steal* (old rhyming slang: *inch = pinch*)

half iron *heterosexual (possibly bi-sexual) who associates with homosexuals* (derived from rhyming slang: *iron hoof = poof*)

half ounce deal (1) buy half an ounce of a drug. (2) when a prisoner swaps a half-ounce of tobacco for a **joint**; see also **deal, phonecard deal**

half-way house accommodation which is half way between institutional life and independent living

HALOW *Help and Advice Line* for prisoners, ex-prisoners, partners, families and friends. There are four HALOWS: the London HALOW offers escorted visits, transport and support for prisoners and their families. The HALOWS in Birmingham, Bristol and Coventry offer support for prisoners' partners (1996)

handful *five year sentence*

handing out babies have to be separated from their mothers after spending up to the first 18 months of their lives in an **MBU**; see also **emergency handout**

handling *handling stolen goods* (contrary to section 22 Theft Act 1968). 'I got done for handling'; see also **buyer, fence, placer, receiver**

handout when prisoner's property is given to a visitor to take away

hang paper *pass dud cheques;* see also **kiter, leafer, paperhanger**

happiness is door-shaped implying that some prison officers are only happy when prisoners are locked in their cells; see also **key happy**

happy *Ecstasy:* see **E**

hard bit *difficult sentence*

hardcore *amyl nitrite* clear or yellow liquid in small bottle. Costs £7 a bottle from sex shops (1996). Can be inhaled from the bottle or a rag. Known as the 'gay drug' because it relaxes the muscles making anal intercourse easier; see also **GBH, LG, liquid gold, locker room, poppers, red rush, rush, thrust, zap**

hard man *tough prisoner*

hard stuff *hard drugs* especially cocaine (see **C**) or heroin (see **H**)

harm *self-harm* formerly self-mutilation

Harry *heroin:* see **H**

harry-carry *suicide* from the Japanese *hari kari* (ritual disembowelling)

hash *hashish:* see generally **marijuana.** Also **hashover** hangover from using hashish; **hash tea** herbal tea containing **cannabis**

60

hatch *window in cell door* through which items may be passed and communication can take place; see **Judas eye, Judas hole**

have it away/have it on your toes *escape:* see **away**

hay see **marijuana**

HBI *house breaking implements*

HCC *health care centre* the prison hospital unit, wing; see also **vet, SMO**

HCO *health care officer*

HCSP *Health Care Service for Prisoners* modern name for the Prison Medical Service (see **PMS**)

head (1) enough cannabis for a single **joint;** see also **bif, bifta, bomber, draw, nightcap, puff, spliff, toke, zoot** (2) 'top dog' prisoner who may intimidate/bully others and run extortion rackets; see also **baron, daddy**

headbanger, head case(1) *mentally ill prisoner* (2) someone who literally bangs his or her head against walls, doors, floors

head office *Prison Service HQ*

heat *harsh interrogation* intense police interest/pressure following a crime

heater revolver (derived from the US gangster lore); see also **gat, rod, shooter**

heaven sent *Ecstasy:* see **E**

heavies, heavy mob (1) officers brought in to deal with riotous behaviour. (2) gang involved in violent or large scale crimes. (3) lesbian prison officers

heavy *armed robbery*

heavy drug *hard drug, narcotic*

hemp see **marijuana**

Henry *heroin:* see **H**

herb see **marijuana**

Her Majesty's pleasure while life imprisonment is the mandatory sentence for murder committed by a person aged 21 or over, if the offender is aged 10 to 17 the equivalent mandatory sentence is detention during Her Majesty's pleasure; see also **custody for life, discretionary life sentence, mandatory life sentence, natural lifer**

HIA *Head of Inmate Activities*

Hibiscus organization that supports women foreign nationals in UK prisons. It has branches in some African and Caribbean countries where it supports families of women in British prisons. Sister organization of the *Female Prisoners Welfare Project* (**FPWP**)

high *under the influence* (usually of drugs or alcohol)

high hat *opium:* see **O**

high wall job *burglary requiring climbing;* see also **cat burglar, dancer, second storey man**

hiker prison officer whose duty it is to be anywhere in the prison as required; see **call sign, NATO** ('TANGO' and 'PAPA'), **ranger, rover;** see generally **screw**

hit (1) *drug injection* or *dose;* see also **bang, fire up, fix, shot.** (2) *contract killing*

hit and get robbing one place then moving on fast to another

hitman *hired killer*

hit the doctor *get prescription drugs* maybe from GPs who visit prison; see also **dog tag, script, reducing script, vet**

HLED *home leave eligibility date* now resettlement licence eligibility date (see **RLED**). 'Home leave' has been replaced by 'release on resettlement licence' for which prisoners serving four years or more become eligible when they reach their parole eligibility date (see **PED**)

HMCIP *Her Majesty's Chief Inspector of Prisons*

HMP (1) *Her Majesty's Prison,* e.g. HMP Wormwood Scrubs. (2) **Her Majesty's pleasure**: see that item.

HMP No You Can't old name for HMP Strangeways, Manchester before the riots and rooftop demonstrations of 1990

HOAI *Home Office Addicts Index* prison medical officers are obliged to report to the Home Office all addicts arriving in their establishments. The Prison Service equivalent of the **DMD** (Drugs Misuse Database) of the Department of Health. The HOAI shows a significantly higher proportion of injecting drugs misusers in the prison population than in the population in general

hobbies list a list for prisoners to enter their leisure activities for **association** times

hock, in hock *pawned items*

hogman someone who silences alarms while a crime is being committed; see also **earwig**

hoisting *shoplifting;* see also **five finger**

holding *in possession of drugs;* see also **carrying.** 'Are you holding?' = 'Got any drugs?'

holding centre premises used to hold people detained as alleged illegal immigrants: see **detainee**

home leave now renamed 'release on resettlement licence' (see **RLED**): when prisoners are allowed out of prison for periods prior to final release, e.g. to make arrangements for accommodation, employment. **Home, Resettlement Leave Board** looks into a prisoner's suitability for home leave

honeymoon *early days of addiction to drugs* especially heroin (see **H**) or cocaine (see **C**)

hooch *contraband liquor* possibly made in prison from leftover fruit, potatoes or rice and hidden to ferment; see also **jungle juice**

hook deliberately get someone addicted to drugs. **hooked** (1) *addicted* (2) *arrested*; see also **nicked**

hooker *prostitute* from a US General of that name who reputedly supplied women to his troops: see **game, on the game**

hop *opium:* see **O**

62

horrors *drug-induced psychosis* a bad drugs experience or effects of giving up a drug habit; see also **DTs** (*delirium tremens*), **bad trip, flashback**

horse *heroin* (derived from US slang): see **H**

hospital officers prison officers with basic nursing training are employed in hospital units

hospital wing used for sick prisoners and (especially in women's prisons) vulnerable prisoners who may be on **Rule 43:** see **HCC, nonce wing, VP, VPU, VP wing, zoo**

hot *suspect*

hot-plate *prison oven* **hot-plate hamster** prison officer who 'gobbles up' food meant for prisoners

hot up someone point them out to the police: see **finger, grass**

hotwire *start a vehicle by short-circuiting the ignition wires;* see also **TWC, twocking**

house block *accommodation for independent living* usually in an open prison

housing benefit changes in housing benefit entitlement in 1996 have had severe repercussions on prisoners who need housing benefit to cover their rent while they are in prison. Remand prisoners on housing benefit can continue to claim for up to 52 weeks. Sentenced prisoners can claim for up to 13 weeks. But this only applies to people likely to serve 13 weeks or less in custody. If they are to serve more than 13 weeks they

are not entitled to any benefit and often lose their accommodation. For prisoners who are mothers of young children reaching the end of their sentence, this can mean there is a long delay before they can take children home again. People with savings of £16,000 or more are not eligible for housing benefit (1996)

Howard League *Howard League for Penal Reform* nation-wide organization working for reform in the penal system and criminal justice process

hug drug *Ecstasy:* see **E**

hump, get the *be depressed;* see also **blackheart**

hurting for *craving drugs;* see also **habit, jones, monkey**

hustler (1) *drug pusher* (2) *prostitute:* see **game, on the game**

hypo *hypodermic syringe* which can be used to inject drugs; see also **spike**

I

ice blue penguins: see **LSD**

ICO *interim care order*

ID *identity* as in **ID card, ID parade.** Proof of ID needs to be produced by visitors to a prison. **ID card** Britain does not have identity cards, an issue which is a recurring theme when law and order is under discussion. Proposals for a limited, voluntary ID card scheme are under consideration by government (1996). **ID parade** *identity parade* a line-up of possible suspects intermingled with ordinary members of the public fitting a similar description so that witnesses or victims can point to the alleged offender

IDPR *Inmate Development Pre-release* programmes run by probation, psychology teams etc. to prepare prisoners for release

IEPS *Incentives and Earned Privileges Scheme* since 1995 prisoners are placed on one of three differential regimes. These are **Basic, Standard** (sometimes sub-divided into Standard 1 and 2) and **Enhanced.** According to which regime they are on, prisoners get certain privileges, e.g. the amount of **private spends** they are allowed; the number of **visits; community visits.** See also **compact, differential regimes, incentive, privileged wing**

implement loss if a tool or implement from workshops goes missing, this is classed as a serious incident and can result in prisoners remaining locked in their cells until it is recovered; see also **tool loss**

IMR *inmate medical record*

in and out man *opportunist burglar;* see also **lightfoot, specking**

in breach *in breach of a court order or ruling* e.g. (1) breach of bail by failing to turn up at court or by breaking conditions of bail such as a requirement to live at a given address. (2) breach of a conditional discharge, probation order, community service order or a suspended sentence of imprisonment

in cell electrics some prisons have electric power points in cells for mains TV, radio etc. Not all have allowed prisoners to use this facility. There is also a current move to curtail the facility (1996); see also **wire up**

in cell sanitation the aim has been to install WCs to end **slopping out** completely

incentive *inducement* to encourage good behaviour: see **IEPS**

in-charge special allowance which can be claimed by officer-instructors left alone in charge of a large group of prisoners where normally there would be another instructor

induction process of explaining the regime and the education and training courses which are on offer at the start of a prison sentence. Prisoners are given an induction pack and sometimes shown videos. In some prisons, new prisoners stay on the **induction wing/block** for several days

inmate *prisoner* often used officially, despite a Prison Reform Trust view that this term is 'offensive Prison Service jargon' and that its use was in decline following the **Woolf report** (*Prison Report,* Prison Reform Trust, Summer 1996)

Inquest national organization which concerns itself with deaths of people in custody, mounts campaigns and gives advice, support and information to relatives and others

in shit street *in big trouble* (also general usage but very common in prison)

inside *in prison:* see **away, clink**

64

inside job *crime committed by, or with the help of, an 'insider'* such as a security guard, watchman, partner, employee or associate. Often used in relation to organizations, insurance swindles, domestic crimes

insider dealing the misuse of financial information to which associates, employees have access; see also **creamer**

Inside Time the only national newspaper for prisoners, issued to all prisons in the UK. A platform which enables prisoners to express their views in letters and articles. Produced by **The New Bridge**

interview report a parole interview is part of the process whereby a prisoner serving more than four years is interviewed by a member of the **Parole Board** to assess his or her suitability for discharge. A report is written on the interview and sent to the parole secretariat, with a copy to the prisoner for any comments

in the frame *under suspicion, investigation*

in the pads *in padded cells.* Contrast **in the strips**

in the safe drugs, money or other contraband items concealed in the anus to avoid detection during a strip search: see **bottling**

in-use *in-use certified normal accommodation* (**C N A**). The maximum number of places that a prison has at any one time; see also **baseline**

IO *instructional officer* a prison officer who is qualified to instruct on courses or workshops; see also **Adidas, CIT**

IP *in possession* there are penalties for possession of contraband in prison, especially drugs. There is an approved list of articles allowed to prisoners (which can be adapted at an individual governor's discretion)

I P R S *Inmate Personal Record System* used to track the progress of prisoners prison to prison, e.g. educational achievements should be so recorded

IPV *inter-prison visit* visit of one prisoner to someone in another prison (usually a relative, partner or sometimes a sibling). Subject to other considerations, this may be allowed once every three months. Both parties have to use up a **VO**

iron, iron hoof *male homosexual* (rhyming slang *hoof = poof*): see **bent, half iron**

Island, the the Isle of Wight, meaning HMP Parkhurst, Albany or Camp Hill

J

jacks *pills* medical not narcotic (rhyming slang: *Jack and Jills = pills*)

jacksie *buttocks, anus, vagina*

Jack the Lad *a bit of a lad, a rogue.* Term used to excuse dubious - possibly criminal - behaviour by young males, usually by relatives or associates (also general usage)

jack up/a jack up (1) *inject/an injection of drugs,* e.g. 'a jack up of

smack'; see also **bang up, hit, shoot up, mainline.** (2) body search

jailbait *girl below the age of consent* for the purposes of sexual intercourse, i.e. 16 in the UK, the main connotation being that the girl appears older and more sexually sophisticated than her years. A 'one strike only' statutory defence is available under which a man can assert that he mistook a girl's age, in effect if he is under 24 and charged with **USI** with a girl aged 13 to 15

jailbird *prisoner;* see also **birdman, con, body, lag, old lag**

jail bollocks *problems* from other prisoners and officers

jailcraft knowledge of the day-to-day running of a prison acquired by a prison officer, often by experience. Many long-serving prison officers consider that the initial training of recruits should include more 'jailcraft'

jailee *jailer* prison officer (the reverse of what 'jailee' ought to signify): see **screw**

jail politician prisoner who stirs up disaffection or manipulates officers. Compare 'barrack room lawyer', a military term now in general use

jamjar *car* (rhyming slang)

jam/jam roll *parole* (rhyming slang)

jammy/jemmy *crowbar* f o r burglary, safebreaking etc

jam sandwich *police car* (from the stripe along its side); see also **black & white, panda, Q boat**

JC *Job Club* before release prisoners may be allowed to visit a Job Club, apply for work and become an **outworker**

JD *juvenile delinquent*

jellies *temazepam* can come in capsule form which may be opened and the jelly-like contents injected by addicts: see **tems;** see also **downers, eggs, green eggs, tranx, wobbly eggs**

jimmy (1) **foil** (rhyming slang: *Jimmy Boyle = foil*) used for smoking heroin: see **H.** Jimmy Boyle was a well-known prisoner, now a journalist and author: see also **olive oil.** (2) **fix** (a dose, often an injection of drugs) (rhyming slang: *Jimi Hendrix = fix*). Jimi Hendrix (deceased) was a leading 1960s reggae guitarist

job *crime* usually a robbery

jobbed/jobber *framed;* see also **fit up, frame up**

Joe Baxi *taxi* (rhyming slang)

Joe Gurr *prison* (rhyming slang *Gurr = stir = Romany for prison*): see **clink**

joey (1) *illicit goods* often a small pack of drugs; see also **bag, bagel, finger, paper, sack, scorebag, w r a p** (2) *a weak prisoner* intimidated by another prisoner and has to obey his or her orders

Johnny letter same as a **Dear J o h n** letter, often ending a relationship

joint *cigarette* m a d e w i t h **marijuana** (hence to roll a **joint,** to smoke a joint); see also **bif**

jones, to have a to be addicted to drugs; see also **habit, hurting, monkey**

joy, joybang one dose of drugs by an occasional drugs user

JR (1) *judge's remand* (convicted but not yet sentenced): 'I've been JRd' means 'I have been put on remand by the judge pending pre-sentence reports'. (2) *judicial review* a prisoner can apply to the High Court for a judicial review: (a) if there are felt to be grounds of impropriety, illegality or irrationality in the way he or she has been treated in prison. A JR will only be undertaken once all other internal prison procedures for complaint and appeal have been exhausted. This form of JR rarely happens and when it does it is mainly concerned with the procedure at an adjudication hearing. (b) a legal remedy, by way of an application to the High Court to challenge the decision of a lower court, tribunal or public officer where it is claimed that proper procedures have not been followed or there has been impropriety

Judas eye/Judas hole *hatch in cell door* through which prisoner can be watched, passed food by officers; see also **hatch**

judge in chambers where part of a case is dealt with *in camera* (i.e. in private, without a jury) rather than in open court

jug (1) *prison* (rhyming slang: *jug and pail = jail*): see **clink**. Also **jugged** *in prison*: see **away, in jug** (2) *bank*

jugging *assault with a jug of boiling water;* see also **boiled**

juggling *drug dealing*

juice   *methadone* a heroin substitute, a synthetic opiate used to treat heroin dependence; see also **meth, reducing script, three day chop**

juicer *collector for a loan shark*

jump bail *run away; see also* **abscond**

jump (1) *sudden attack* (often rape); see also **junior jumper** (2) *sexual intercourse*

jungle bunny *black person* (racist)

jungle juice *strong, usually cheap, alcohol;* see also **hooch**

junk *heroin*: see **H**. Can mean any illicit drug. **junkie** *drug addict* (also in general use)

junior jumper *underage rapist* the former legal presumption that a boy below the age of 14 was incapable of sexual intercourse and thus of rape has been abolished

JUSTICE organization that lobbies for reform of the criminal justice process and sometimes helps in miscarriage of justice cases

just-in-caser *getaway car;* see also **skid   artist, stoppo driver, wheelman**

K

K khat, green leaves of the shrub *Catha edulis* chewed across East Africa a narcotic, hallucinogenic, stimulant; see also **qat, qaadka** seemingly not illegal in the UK

k, key *kilo* of drugs

kanga *prison officer* (rhyming slang: *kangaroo = screw*); see **screw**

kardomah *officers' mess* from 1950s/1960s chain of tea rooms

Kate Bush see **marijuana**. Bush is a common word for marijuana. Kate Bush is a well-known singer

kazi *WC;* see also **carzie, kharzie, khazi**

KB *knockback* a setback, e.g if a prisoner loses an appeal, is refused **parole** or is told that his or her next review for release will not be heard for some time; see also **blank**. Can also refer to a shock from receiving a letter saying a relationship is over; see **Dear John, Johnny letter**

keep your head *down stay out of trouble.* Common phrase used at end of letters from prisoners; see also **stay safe**

kennel see **cell**

kettle *wrist watch*

key *prison officer:* see **screw**

key happy fond of locking up prisoners in cells; see also **happiness is door shaped**

khat see **K**

khazi *WC;* see also **carzie, kazi, kharzie**

kicking trying to end a drugs habit; see also **cold turkey, withdrawing**

kick off (1) *widescale misbehaviour* (2) *kick a cell door* when angry at locking in; can mean 'wrecking' a cell

kick out *leave a gang*

kick ten bells (of shit) out of someone *beat up, very seriously;* see also **GBH**

kif see **marijuana**

Kilburn *police diary* (rhyming slang *Kilburn Priory = diary*)

kiss arse *crawl* to get your way

kisser *mouth, face;* see also **mush**

kit (1) *drug equipment;* see also **fit, gear, outfit, works.** (2) *prison letter* (3) *contraband goods* (4) *necessities* a male prisoner is given clothes sufficient for one week. Women prisoners can wear their own clothes unless they are working on certain tasks e.g. the kitchens (see also **kit change**). Prison Rules list objects that prisoners are allowed to keep in their cells, but this is subject to the discretion of individual **governors;** see also **IP**

kit change (1) *place where soiled clothing is exchanged* usually the **bath house** (2) *changing clothes* Also **kit officer** i.e. who hands out **kit**

kite *forged cheque* **kiter** *user of forged cheques/credit cards;* see also **lay a kite, fly a kite, laydown merchant, leafer, paperhanger, penman, scratcher, slinger, scratcher.** Also used as a verb: **kiting** passing forged cheques

klep *kleptomaniac* compulsive thief

knockback see **KB**; see also **blank**

knocker *confidence trickster* posing as a door-to-door salesman. see also **drummer**

knock off (1)*steal* (2) *arrest* **knocked off** (1) *stolen* (2) *arrested* see also **nicked**

knock out drops *sedative* including when added to someone's drink so he or she can be robbed, assaulted whilst drugged. Compare **fraggle juice, liquid cosh, loopy juice, Mickey Finn**

knuckle sandwich *punch with the fist* usually on the jaw, mouth

KPI *key performance indicators* the Prison Service has eight KPIs. A main goal is to maintain good order and discipline (**GOAD**) and a safe environment. KPIs should show improvements year on year

Kremlin, the *Scotland Yard* after the Russian government building: see **brains**

L

L coe I SD

LA *lesbian activities* forbidden in prison; women publicly showing physical affection to each other can be put on a disciplinary charge (under **GOAD**) though in some prisons officers turn a blind eye

Labour 1, 2, 3 *classifications of levels of work* prisoners are felt to be capable of, e.g. Labour 1 means any kind of work, however heavy; Labour 3 is the lightest work, thought suitable for pregnant prisoners. A **labour control officer** usually interviews and advises prisoners about available prison jobs. **Labour change**: see **change**

of **labour form**. Also **Labour movement, parade** instructions over tannoy that prisoners are to go to work locations; see also **NAL**

lady *cocaine* because it is supposed to be a female aphrodisiac: see **C, girl**

laid down *remanded in custody*

lag *prisoner* **old lag** *regular* possibly someone who is institutionalised. Old lag usually reserved for repeat petty offenders as opposed to people serving long sentences; see also **con, birdman, body, jailbird**

Kiter

lagging *serving sentence in prison* (originally 'lagging' meant transportation); also used for a sentence over two years; see also **beggar's lagging, tramp's lagging**

lam, on the *on the run:* see **away**

landing (1) *group of cells* on a wing; see also **spur**. (2) *walkway* in a prison hall or on a wing; see also **bridge** (3) *the level* some prisons divide prisoners on differential regimes by level, so that, e.g. the top landing will house prisoners on an **Enhanced** regime (see **differential regimes**). **Landing officer** in charge of a landing

Language Line *telephone interpreting service* which provides translators in approximately 140 languages 24 hours a day. Prison staff can tap into Language Line to talk to prisoners whose mother tongue is not English. However the service is felt by some governors to be beyond their budget and they do not subscribe to it

Largactil shuffle *unsteady walk* e.g. of a prisoner on heavy medication; see also **muppet shuffle** *Largactil* is the brand name for the anti-psychotic drug *chlorpromazine*

laughing Buddha see **LSD**

laundromat *business front* for processing ('laundering') illicit gains, usually cash; see also **front man, laydown merchant**

law, the *police:* see **Bill**

lay a kite *pass a forged cheque;* see also **fly a kite**

laydown merchant *distributor of forged money;* see also **kiter,**

leafer, paperhanger, penman, scratcher, slinger

LBB/LBW *locks, bolts and bars/locks, bolts and windows* daily procedure whereby prison officers routinely check each cell to see that a prisoner is not able to escape

LDR *latest date of release* old term now replaced by **SED** (sentence expiry date)

leaf *cocaine:* see **C**

leafer *cheque* usually fraudulent or forged; see also **kiter, laydown merchant, paperhanger, penman, scratcher, slinger**

Learmont Report *report* by General Sir John Learmont into an escape by three prisoners from HMP Parkhurst in 1994. He also reviewed implementation of recommendations in the **Woodcock Report** for improving security at HMP Whitemoor, following escapes there

leaves *cigarette/drugs papers;* see also **papers, Rizlas (after the brand name), skins, wafers**

Lebanese gold *cannabis:* see **marijuana**

LED *licence expiry date* prisoners who have been released on licence remain under supervision at least until the three-quarters point of the whole sentence. This date is known as the LED. But even after this point, a prisoner is at risk of recall to prison until his or her sentence expiry date (**SED**)

left hand to left hand *a method of attaching handcuffs;* see also **cross-cuffing, shackles**

legal aid means-tested system whereby accused people may be provided with a lawyer to represent them. **legal aid officer** prison officer who assists prisoners concerning legal advice

legal letter *a prisoner's letter to or from his or her solicitor* this must not be opened unless prison authorities suspect it is being misused, in which case this happens in the presence of the prisoner. Both correspondents should write 'Rule 37A' on the envelope to ensure confidentiality. Other envelopes are routinely opened, but letters are not normally read; see also **OL, SL**

legals *lawyers* as in 'I'd let the legals look at that'

legal visit lawyers are allowed to visit clients in prison without using a visiting order (see **VO**). Legal visits can be made at any time and last as long as necessary, though they sometimes have to be booked in advanced for security purposes and so that a room can be made available

legger/done a legger *escaped:* see **away**

leggner *prison sentence of 12 months:* see **stretch**

lemon and limes *Ecstasy:* see **E**

lemon barley *cocaine:* see **C**

level money exact multiple of £100 (from car trader jargon)

LF scam *long firm scam* setting up a firm, fraudulently ordering supplies, then claiming the business has gone under and keeping and selling the supplies

without paying for them, usually disappearing also; **LF gear** = proceeds of LF scam

L G *liquid gold* amyl nitrite: see **hardcore**

lib *liberty* 'It's a downright lib!'

Liberty new name for the National Council for Civil Liberties

liberty clothing if a prisoner does not have suitable clothes to wear on release, the prison has an obligation to provide these; see generally **discharge**

licence/out on licence discharged early on licence and under supervision; see also **life licence**

licking/licking shit *licking rocks* of **crack** cocaine. The effect last between 30 seconds and two minutes

lid 22 grammes of **marijuana**

LIDS *Local Inmate Database System*

lie-down *spell on the block;* see also **twenty-eight day lie down**

lifeboat *commutation of sentence.* Also used to describe a retrial, a free pardon

lifer *prisoner serving a life sentence;* see also **L-plater.** Also **life for life** where a lifer has been told that he or she will never be released (sometimes written **life 4 life**); see also **natural lifer; lifer governor** officer with overall responsibility for life sentence prisoners. Official title is **Life Sentence Liaison Governor**; see also **LLO, LMU; life sentence plan** all **lifers** have a plan for their sentence which will include looking at the reasons for their crime(s) and how these should be addressed, annual reviews, progress reports etc; **life licence** a **lifer** cannot be released until the end of the 'tariff' period. In a mandatory life sentence for murder, the tariff is decided upon by the Home Secretary with advice from the trial judge and the Lord Chief Justice. At the end of the tariff period the Home Secretary has to consider the recommendation of the Parole Board before release can take place. The lifer may then be released on a licence which remains in force for the rest of his or her life. At first the conditions of the licence may mean the released prisoner has to stay in a hostel and keep in close touch with the probation officer. These conditions may be relaxed after several years following release. But at any time the licence can be revoked and the person returned to prison. The same applies to discretionary lifers except that the tariff is decided by the trial judge and at the end of the tariff period release decisions are made by the **Parole Board**

ligature, to to self-harm by tying a ligature (such as a cord, scarf or wire) tightly round the neck until almost strangled. **ligature free cell** cell in which all practicable efforts have been made to eliminate the means of making a ligature

lightfoot *sneak burglar;* see also **in and out man, specking**

lights out after **lockup**, when prisoners on evening **association** are returned to their cells. The cell light is sometimes turned off from the outside

limited alerts measure used to provide staff for an emergency

line (1) *snort of a narcotic,* e.g. cocaine: see **C**. Comes from practice of setting out cocaine or any other drug in powder form in thin lines on a mirror or glass with a razorblade; see also **Patsy Cline, rails, toot** as in 'Want a line of Charlie?' (2) lines of communication with other cells made of strips of sheets knotted together. Prisoners use these to pass e.g. **roll-ups** outside the windows. Hence 'Giz a line!'. Compare **flying pasty, swing**

line-up *identity parade;* see also **ID**

liquid cosh *tranquilizers, sedatives* to keep prisoners quiet or used in pursuance of crime; see also **fraggle juice, knock out drops, loopy juice, Mickey Finn**

liquid e *gamma hydroxybutyrate* (see **GHB**); also called **GBH, hardcore, liquid gold, liquid x**

listeners prisoners trained by the Samaritans to act as counsellors to fellow prisoners. They often wear a badge to identify themselves; see also **ears**

LLO see **lifer liaison officer**

LMU *lifer management unit*

loaded *high on drugs*

loan shark someone who lends out money at extortionately high interest rates; see also **double back, double bubble, juicer, two for one**

local nick *local prison,* i.e. local to the court, to which prisoners are normally sent on remand or before

72

being sent to other prisons to serve their sentences

local purchase provisions that prisoners cannot buy in the prison **c a n t e e n** but which can be purchased in local shops. Security restrictions following the **Woodcock Report** and **Learmont Report** have restricted this practice

local recruitment arrangement whereby prisons now recruit staff locally

location where a prisoner lives, officially listed as the letter/number of **cell, landing** and **wing**

lockdown when all prisoners are locked in cells for a rollcall check

locker room *amyl nitrite:* see **hardcore**

lockhand *a form of repetitive strain injury or arthritis* a physical complaint peculiar to prison warders from constantly turning keys in locks

locking in a form of industrial action taken by prison officers to suppress freedom of **association**

locking out action taken by the **POA** to reduce overcrowding to the **CNA** by refusing entry to prisoners brought to the prison by police, bailiffs and immigration officers. This happened during the industrial disputes of the 1980s and resulted in prisoners being returned to police or other approved cells temporarily

lockup (1) when prisoners are locked in their cells for much of the day. (2) the process of locking into cells; see also **bang up, key happy, shut down**

lollied *informed upon* (rhyming slang: *lollipopped = shopped*): see **grass**

lolly *money* (rhyming slang: *lollipop = drop = tip*): see **bread**

long term has traditionally meant a prisoner serving more than four years (men) and three years (women). However, the Criminal Justice Act 1991 defined long term prisoners, *male or female*, as those serving four years or more. **long-termer** prisoner with such a sentence; see also **on tour**

looks like rain *about to be arrested*

loopy juice strong medication, tranquilizers; see also **fraggle juice, knock out drops, liquid cosh, Mickey Finn**

LOP *loss of privileges*

loppy *lousy* infested with lice; see also **Rosie Lee**

lose privs *lose privileges,* e.g. following an adverse **adjudication**

Lou Reed *amphetamines* (rhyming slang: *Lou Reed - speed*): see **A.** Lou Reed was a one-time singer with the American cult band Velvet Underground

love doves/love hearts *Ecstasy:* see **E**

love, light of *prison governor* (rhyming slang: *love = guv*)

L-plate(r) *life-sentence prisoner:* see **lifer, natural**

LRC *Local Review Committee* to consider **parole** applications. Phased out with the introduction of the new system of early release in the Criminal Justice Act 1991

LSD *lysergic acid diethylamide* A synthetic hallucinogenic drug derived from ergot, a type of fungus. £2.50-£5 (1996) per tablet or **blotter** (see **tab**), a piece of blotting paper a quarter of the size of a standard postage stamp impregnated with the drug. Other common names include:

> **acid, Bart Simsons (Barts), Bartmans, batmans, black micro, black Russians, blotter, blue ice, blue stars, Flintstones (flints), funky yellows, funny papers, ghostbusters, green micro, green penguins, ice blue penguins, laughing Buddha, lucy, microdots, orange magics, power rangers, purple gnomes, red dragons, rhubarbs, Russian roulettes, smileys, sonics, strawberries, sugar, stars, supermans, tabs, trips, turtles, white light, world cups, ying yangs, zig and zags**

Names often depend on the design of the **tabs**

LTI *long term inmate*

LTRB *long term review board* which checks on a prisoner's progress through a long term sentence

lucy see **LSD**. As in the title of the 1960s John Lennon and Paul McCartney composition for The Beatles, 'Lucy in the Sky with Diamonds'

M

M *morphine* the best known narcotic analgesic drug (pain killer) derived from the unripe seeds of the opium poppy, The euphoric effects are addictive and lead to its abuse. Craving leads to a need for increased amounts. Other common names include: **cube, dolly, GOM, Miss Emma, morph, O, white nurse, white stuff**

M and Ms *drugs in pill form* After the brand name for children's sweets

Macintyre *fire* (rhyming slang)

magic mushrooms, magics *hallucinogenic mushrooms.* A species containing the substance *psilocybin.* There are many varieties, but Liberty Cap is the best known. They grow wild all over Britain and cost £1 or so per 20-30 if sold; not unlawful to pick or use raw, but they become so if prepared in any way; see also **mushies, shrooms, wonderveg**

magic roundabout when a troublesome prisoner is moved from prison to prison; see also **ghosted, shared misery circuit, twenty-eight day lie down.** After the TV animation *The Magic Roundabout*

main (1) *the general prison population* (as opposed to the **VPU** or the **block** (2) *main vein* into which drugs are injected. Sometimes used as a verb: **to mainline.** Also **mainliner** addict who injects into the main vein; see also **tie off, tracking.** Contrast **skin popping**

make a break *attempt an escape* from police or prison custody: see **away**

make one *take part in an illicit plot in prison* usually an escape plan

make one out *escape*: see **away**

male estate see **estate**

Mallet, The HMP Shepton Mallet, Somerset

man, the addicts' name for a drugs dealer

mandatory life sentence offenders convicted of murder receive a mandatory life sentence and the tariff period is set by the Home Secretary. When this period has expired the Home Secretary may release the prisoner if the Parole Board so recommends, but on release, such prisoners remain on licence for the rest of their lives and are subject to recall if their behaviour suggests they might again endanger the public; see also **custody for life, discretionary life sentence, lifer, Her Majesty's pleasure**

Mandy *Mandrax* a barbiturate used especially to speed up and heighten the effects of alcohol. Costs £5 per tablet (1996)

m a n o r (1) *police division* (2) *territory* geographical area 'ruled' by a gang

marijuana the flowering tops and dried leaves of the female Indian **hemp** plant *cannabic sativa*. Contains the active ingredient THC (*tetrahydro cannabinol*) which is found also in **cannabis resin (hashish)**. The resin is made from the oil of the plant and is sold in block form. The chopped leaves are usually smoked as a **joint** or reefer but can be drunk as tea or eaten in food. It is a generic central nervous system depressant. Both marijuana and cannabis cost £120 an ounce, but are usually sold by the quarter ounce for £30, or an **eighth** for £15, £8 for a sixteenth

Common names for **cannabis** include:

Afghan, brick, gold, gold seal, hash, hashish, Lebanese gold, Moroccan Black, red seal, resin, rocky, rocky black, slate, soap, soap bar, squidgy black, zerozero

Common names for **marijuana** include:

basil, Basil Brush, blow, bush, catweed, dope, ganja, grass, gunja, hay, hemp, herb, Kate Bush, kif, parsley, pot, pox, puff, purple haze, skunk, superweed, tack, tea, Thai, Thailand grass, Thaisticks, weed, whacky backy

Mars bar *scar* (rhyming slang)

M a r v *Marvetol* a laxative for children which is sometimes mixed with **cocaine**

Mary-Jane cocaine (rhyming slang): see **C**. Users planning to buy might e.g. ask 'Is Mary-Jane coming out tonight?'

match, matchbox half an ounce of **marijuana**

MAXL *maximum potential licence period*

MBU/M and BU *mother and baby unit* there are four MBUs in the women's prison system (1996) taking approximately 70 babies and young children. At HMPs Holloway and New Hall, babies can stay with their mothers until the age of nine months, and at HMP Askham Grange and HMP Styal the limit is 18 months. Mothers who wish to keep their babies with them are rarely separated at nine months, but are transferred to one of the longer-stay MBUs. However, babies can be sent out of the prison if the mother is in breach of prison discipline and has to be segregated. The law does not allow a baby to be locked into a cell; see also **handing out, emergency handout**

McKenzie Friend a party to legal proceedings in court may ask a friend to be with him or her for the purpose of assisting, and similarly at a governor's adjudication. The friend may take notes and give advice, though he or she is only allowed to address others with the leave of the court. From a litigant called McKenzie who took his own case to court with the help of a friend and without a lawyer. It is now accepted that such unqualified assistance should be allowed unless the arrangement is such as to interfere with the interests of justice

M D T *mandatory drugs testing* requires prisoners to provide a urine sample for testing purposes, and it is a disciplinary offence for a prisoner to use a controlled drug without appropriate medical authorisation. MDT involves choosing prisoners to supply a specimen. Testing is carried out under a degree of supervision to avoid substitute specimens being supplied. Refusal to supply a sample is a disciplinary offence, as is substitution of samples, and prisoners can be segregated while samples are taken. Every prison is required to test 10 per cent of prisoners at random each month but the Rules provide for other testing, e.g. if there is 'reasonable suspicion', or on reception into a prison, or frequent tests of persistent drugs misusers. Called **piss test** by prisoners; see also **taking the piss, VTU**

meat box *prison transport:* see **Black Maria**

meat eater *corrupt policeman*

meat rack *where male prostitutes operate*

meat wagon *prison transport:* see **Black Maria**

medium term traditionally refers to length of sentence, i.e. 18 months to three years for women and 18 months to four years for men. But see the comments about the true position under **long term prisoner**

mesc *mescaline* a hallucinogenic and psychedelic drug obtained from the Mexican peyote cactus. Similar effect to **LSD**

mess *prison officer's dining room:* see also **kardomah**

Met *Metropolitan Police*

meth *methadone* heroin substitute: a synthetic narcotic opiate used to treat opiate dependence. Some prison medical officers refuse to allow prisoners to continue on their prescriptions of methadone; see also **juice, reducing scripts**

mic, micro, microdots tablet form of **LSD**; see also **black micro**

Mickey Finn *knock out drug* used to tranquilize disruptive prisoners: usually contains alcohol mixed with chloral hydrate; see also **fraggle, knock out drops, liquid cosh, loopy juice**

midnight mass *informer* (rhyming slang *mass = blade of grass*): see **grass**

mileage *previous convictions;* see also **form, former, pc, previous, record, sheet, yellow sheet**

miln up *lock a cell door* (from the Miln brand name for locks); see also **bang up, chubb up, dub up**

mind-blowing *hallucinogenic,* e.g. **LSD**. As in 'blow your mind'

minder *bodyguard*

Minnesota Method *US style drugs rehabilitation programme* sometimes used in the UK

MINL *minimum licence period*

mint rocks *socks* (rhyming slang); see also **almonds**

mints *Ecstasy:* see **E**

Miss prisoners customarily call any woman officer or visitor 'Miss', just as they usually call male officers and visitors **'Boss'**

Miss Emma *morphine;* see **M**

mixed house a **wing, landing** or **house block** where **long term** and **short term** prisoners live side by side

MO *medical officer*

mong *idiot;* see also **bagel, bagle, balloon, cuckoo, div, fraggle, fruit, fruitcake, headbanger, headcase, muppet, nugget**

monkey (1) **have the monkey on your back** *addicted to drugs;* see also **habit, hurting, jones.** (2) *hot potato* buck passing. (3) *padlock* (4) *£500*

monster *child molester* or other pervert or sex offender: see **animal**

moodies, moody Es *fake Ecstasy tablets* (see **E**) such as vitamin pills. From **doing a moody** meaning acting falsely

moon (1) *calendar month* 'I got 24 moon'. (2) *bare the behind*

Moor, the HMP Dartmoor

Moroccan Black see **marijuana**

morphing *taking morphine:* see **M**

movements prisoners coming into or leaving a prison; see also **labour movement/parade**

Mr Big *leader of a gang* (US origin)

Mr Busy prison officer 'with attitude'; see also **Rambo, screw**

MT *medical transfer* generally from prison to the segregation unit of a secure hospital for psychiatric observation

M to F *Monday to Friday*

muck truck *food trolley;* see also **cob, cobitis, slop time, trolley route**

mud *opium:* see **O**

MUFTI *minimum use of force tactical intervention* **muftied** dragged down to the **block.** Also **Mufti Squad** officers who remove disruptive prisoners. MUFTI may also occur in relation to a **cell spin**

mugging *street robbery*

mugshot *head and shoulders photograph;* see also **gallery, rogues gallery**

mule *drugs courier;* see also **courier, finger**

mump *take a bribe:* s e e **backhander**

muppet *idiot* from the American animated TV series *The Muppet Show;* see also **bagel, bagle, balloon, cuckoo, fraggle, fruitcake, mong, nugget.** Also **muppet shuffle** unsteady walk after taking tranquilisers; see also **Largactil shuffle, zombie medicine.** Also (1) **muppet shop** *prison workshop:* because of the mindless nature of many of the tasks; see also **noddyshop** (2) **muppet house** *psychiatric unit* or *mental hospital;* see also **PCCU, Fraggle Rock, Hospital Unit**

mush (1) *mate* especially among male prisoners; see also **chaffy** (2) *face;* see also **kisser**

mushies see **magic mushrooms**

muster *tally, counting up of prisoners* in open prisons prisoners have to attend all meals in the dining room three times a day for 'muster'. They can then leave the room without eating the meal if they please; see also **roll check**

mutiny prisoners who take part in a prison disturbance can be prosecuted for mutiny

N

NA *Narcotics Anonymous* non-professional self-help group of recovering addicts who are learning to live without drugs. Hold meetings in prisons and offer ongoing help on release with their weekly meetings. Also run prisoner pen pal schemes

NACRO *National Association for the Care and Resettlement of Offenders* organization that helps ex-prisoners find work and accommodation and also provides a range of other services for offenders and ex-offenders

NAL *non-associated labour* a form of punishment; see also **seg, Labour**

NAPV *National Association of Prison Visitors* group that co-ordinates volunteer prison visitors and promotes prison visiting. There are about 1,400 prison visitors, more or less half of them men and half women. Prisoners can apply to their **landing officer** or **prison visitor liaison officer** for such a visit, which will be confidential. Not to be confused with the **Board of Visitors** (see **BOV**)

name badges the wearing of name badges by prison officers and other staff has been the cause of a long-standing and still continuing dispute; see also **badges**

nance *effeminate or homosexual man:* see **bent**

narc/nark (1) *informer* from coppers' nark. Thought to derive from Romany word '*nak*' meaning 'nose'; see generally **grass.** (2) *narcotics informer*

Narco, the *narcotics squad*

National, the the National Transport system between prisons. Civillian buses rather than cubicled vans move prisoners, usually every Wednesday; see also **on tour with the National.** Contrast **Black Maria** etc

Nasty, the *heroin:* see **H**

NATO phonetic alphabet call signs used by prison officers and police on their walkie-talkies are based on this alphabet. The meanings are the same in all prisons, e.g.:

FOXTROT = farms and gardens; HOTEL = hospital; VICTOR = duty governor; ZULU = dog handler; X-Ray = vehicle escort; GOLF = gate; YANKEE = staff, e.g canteen; WHISKEY = Works; TANGO and PAPA are spare officers on patrol and each has a number so they can call each other: 'TANGO 1 to PAPA 2' etc

natural lifer prisoner who has been told that he or she will never be released: see **lifer, life for life**

nature of charge euphemism for vulnerable prisoners, especially those convicted of child abuse or child murder. Because of the risk of attacks by other prisoners, **VPs** are routinely advised to 'lie' about their offences; see also **deps, Rule 43, Schedule One offence**

NEC *National Executive Committee* (of the **POA**)

necking swallowing drugs during a visit to be retrieved later by excretion; see also **closed visits, crutching, downing, gob grabbing**

negs *child neglect* usually in relation to women. Nowadays a rather old-fashioned term

nemby/nembies *Nembutal* a sedative: see **barb, barbs**

NEPO *new entrant prison officer*

next door neighbour *prisoner in the next cell*

nevis *seven month* or *seven year sentence* (backslang)

New Bridge, The Founded in 1956 to create links between the offender and the community. Befriends men, women and young people in prison through a national network of volunteers, by finding employment for ex-offenders and by encouraging the public to accept the need to reintegrate ex-offenders into the community. Produces the prison newspaper *Inside Time*

new fish *new prisoner;* see also **first bird, fish, star**

New Yorkers *Ecstasy:* see **E**

NFA *no fixed abode* a common response during reception procedures when prisoners are asked for their home address

NIC *nominal index card*

nice bit sentence of three years plus

nice little earner (1) *job* usually unlawful, that makes easy money. (2) *good result* in court verdict or following a prison request (see **app**); see also **earner, result, squeeze**

nick (1) *steal* (2) *police station* (3) *prison* ; see also **away, clink.** Also **nick culture** *prison culture,* e.g. loyalty code whereby prisoners will not betray another. (4) *arrest*

nicked, nicking (1) *arrested* caught, apprehended; see also **bagged, captured, collared, get a fall, grabbed, knocked off, on the pavement, popped, pulled, sneezed, tucked up.** (2) *placed on report* for breach of prison rules and given a governor's **adjudication;** see also **telegram.** (3) *stolen*

nick 'em and stick 'em *a hardline prison officer* only interested in disciplining prisoners and confining them in cells: 'He's a real nick 'em and stick 'em type': see generally **screw**. Also used in relation to the police

nicker *pound* 'That cost me fifty nicker'

nightcap *cannabis cigarette:* see **bif, marijuana**

night patrol/night ranger prison officer on night duty (similarly night **kanga**, night **screw** etc.); see also **dark day**

night sanitation in the past, prisoners had to use plastic chamber pots and 'slop out' each morning into a communal sluice. Some prisons allowed prisoners to be given access to the hall after lock-up for a brief time during the night to use the wing WCs. Increasingly, there is in-cell sanitation; see also **flying pasty, recess, shit parcel, slop out**

Nineteen-eighty cell a secure cell used for prisoners at risk to themselves or other people. This refers to the '1980 form' in prison regulations completed before such a cell can be used for a maximum period of 28 days: see **block**

nish *nothing* 'I got nish' e.g. no cigarettes, drugs or tobacco

Nitto! *warning shout;* see also **eye eye!, on top!**

noah's ark *informer* (rhyming slang *ark = nark = informer*); also reversed as **'oah's nark**, a Spoonerism with a double meaning of (1) *informer* and (2) in its

expanded form **whore's nark**; see also **grass**

nod out *fall asleep* usually meaning while using drugs

noddy *police motorbike* after 'Noddy', the naive children's character created by Enid Blyton

noddyshop *prison workshop* because work there is said to be basic (capable of being undertsood by 'Noddy', the naive children's character created by Enid Blyton), dull and repetitive; see also **muppet shop**

nonce *rapist, child molester, pervert or other sex offender:* see **animal**. Also **nonce wing** *Vulnerable Prisoners' Unit;* see also **Rule 43, VPU, VP wing, zoo**

normal location mixing with the general population of a prison, i.e. not on the block or in a **VPU** on **Rule 43**

NOS *Not Off Sanctions,* i.e. still under a disciplinary order depriving the prisoner privileges. 'They kept issuing me with NOS!'

nose *informer* (Romany *nak = nose = narc/nark*): see **grass**

nose, nose candy *cocaine:* see **C**

nosebag *plastic bag for sniffing glue;* see also **glue, stickup, spray**

nosh *meal time;* see also **cob, cobitis, muck truck, slop time, trolley route**

NPD *non parole date* prisoners with sentences of 4 years and over are released after two thirds of their sentence (their NPD), but may be released at any time from the half-

80

way point; see also **DCR, on licence**

NS *nursing sister*

nudger *pickpocket;* see also **dipper, diver, fingers, whizz, whizzer, whizz mob**

nugget *stupid or mentally handicapped person;* see also **bagel, bagle, balloon, cuckoo, div, fraggle, fruit, fruitcake, headbanger, headcase, mong, muppet**

number see **prison number**

Number 1 governor i.e. *The* Prison Governor. The head governor, sometimes called the **governing governor;** see also **guv, love** (i.e. *light of love*)

numbers (1) **getting the/waiting for the** prison officer expression for making sure all prisoners are accounted for. With increasingly high security in prisons, the 'numbers' will be announced over a central tannoy system and prisoners in every section of the prison will have to wait until the go-ahead is given to unlock cells; see also **CAC3, control room, first unlock** (2) **numbers** *sex offenders* child molesters, perverts etc (because they are on **Rule** [number] **43**): see **animal.** Also **numbered** put on **Rule 43**

numb out show the effects of **crack** cocaine or other drugs

nutted off *sent to a secure psychiatric hospital* e.g. Broadmoor

NVQ *National Vocational Qualification* the modular nature of these courses makes them especially suited to prisoners, who

may well be **short term** or moving from one prison to another (see **ghosted)**

O

O *opium* a narcotic drug derived from unripe seeds of poppy plant. Other common names include **black, brown stuff, button, high hat, hop, mud, tar.** Morphine (see **M**) is a derivative of opium

'oah's nark *informer* from Noah's Ark. Also expanded to **whore's nark;** see generally **grass**

OCAU *Observation, Classification and Allocation Unit* on **reception,** sentenced adult men (aged 21 and over) will be sent to this unit where it is decided which category they should be placed in and where they should serve their sentences: see **Cat A** etc.

OD, to OD (1) *overdose, to overdose* usually on hard drugs. 'He OD'd on **heroin'.** (2) *ordinary diet* i.e. not a **special diet** on health or religious grounds

oily, oily rag *cigarette* (rhyming slang *rag = fag = ciqarette*). Could be from oily hands of workmen: see **bif**

Old Bill *the police:* see **Bill**

Old D *Old Dear, Old Darlin'* mother

OL *ordinary letter* contrast **legal letter, special letter**

old man the **governing governor;** see also **guv, love** (i.e. *light of love*)

olive/olive oil *silver foil* used for smoking heroin: see **H** (rhyming slang: *olive oil = foil*); see also **jimmy**

olly *amphetamines* (rhyming slang: *Oliver Reed = speed*): see **A**. Oliver Reed is a film actor

om *Ecstasy:* see **E**

Ombudsman *Prisons Ombudsman* the official appointed to deal with the final stage of any prisoner's grievance. The post was established in 1994 following the recommendations of the Woolf Report (1990) on prison disturbances. The Ombudsman can make recommendations to the **Director General** of the Prison Service or to the Home Secretary. A prisoner should only write to the Ombudsman if he or she has a problem that cannot be resolved in the prison, or if wishing to challenge a decision by the governor

omega *Ecstasy:* see **E**

on a dab on a criminal charge or a prison disciplinary charge

on a pension *bribed:* see **backhander**

on circuit *in transit between jails* officialese; see also **ghosted, magic roundabout, on the ghost train, on tour, on tour with the National, sent to ghost town, shanghaied, shared misery circuit, shipped out**

one away! prison officers' alarm call when a prisoner escapes

one on *new arrival on the wing*

one-er £100

one off escaped (see **away**), gone to the hospital, dead, or off the wing for any other reason

Ones *cells on the ground floor* of a prison. In some prisons those prisoners considered to cause the greatest disciplinary problems are kept on the Ones; see also **Twos, Threes, Fours, Fives**

on licence prisoners are released on licence under the early release provisions and temporarily e.g. on compassionate grounds

on numbers on **Rule 43** a prisoner who has asked to be segregrated for his or her own protection under Prison Rule 43 will be assumed by other prisoners to have committed, e.g. a sex offence or abusing/harming a child: see **animal, on the Rule.** But a prisoner may be on Rule 43 for other reasons such as fear of reprisals; see also **deps**

on report when a prison officer believes a prisoner has committed an offence against prison discipline he or she can place the prisoner on report. The prisoner is given a Notice of Report and a form explaining the **adjudication** procedure. This should happen within 48 hours of the alleged offence; see also **nicked, telegram**

on the book *prisoner who is a security risk;* see also **A-List, E-List, E-man, patches**

on the creep someone who wanders round work places, changing rooms etc. to see what he or she can steal; see also **creeper**

on the ghost train *sent to another prison without warning* usually overnight or early in the morning ('spirited away'): see **ghosted**

on the lam *escaped* on the run: see **away**

on the move *about to do a crime* usually burglary

on the needle *on heroin:* see **H**

on the ones and twos see **on numbers**

on the out the world outside prison

on the pavement *arrested in the street:* see **nicked**

on the plastic stealing and falsely using credit cards; see **doing cards, photogenic**

on the rock on **crack** cocaine; see also **stone, wash**

on the rule see **on numbers**

on the social *on social security* receiving state benefits

on the sick *receiving sick pay*

on the sleeve *caught injecting drugs*

on the take *taking bribes* especially of corrupt prisoner officers or police officers: see **backhander**

on tick *on credit* usually meaning drugs, tobacco; see also **double back, two for one.** Originally from the chalk mark on the slate behind a bar or counter. General usage, but special nuances in prison

on top! *warning shout,* e.g. that an officer is nearby; see also **eye eye!, nitto!**

on tour with the National *moving from prison to prison,* especially if serving a long sentence; see also **magic roundabout, National Transport**

on your toes *escaping/on the run:* see **away**

OP *own protection* form of **Rule 43** whereby a vulnerable prisoner (see **VP**) such as a child molester or someone in debt to other prisoners applies (see **app**) to be segregated

open prison prison to which **Cat D** prisoners may be sent: prisoners who can reasonably be trusted to serve their sentences in less secure open conditions. Certain prisoners, e.g. foreign national drugs importers, are no longer allowed to be in open prison as some have absconded. Some prisoners in open conditions are nearing the end of a long sentence, some may have committed a 'white collar crime' such as fraudulent accounting and are not considered a security risk

open visit (OV) when the prisoner is allowed to sit with visitors around a table. Contrast **closed visit**

orange magics see **LSD**

orderly *prisoner trusted to do a prison job* often some form of minor administration in the prison e.g. education orderly, kitchen orderly, library orderly. There is a small extra payment, e.g. 80p a week; see also **red band, trusty**

orderly officer *officer in day-to-day charge*

OSA *Official Secrets Act*

ounce of tobacco or drugs, though expensive drugs like cocaine (see

83

C) are usually sold in quarters, eighths or sixteenths

outfit (1) *drugs equipment;* see also **fit, gear, works** (2) *escape tackle*

out of it, out of my head, out of my skull *high* confused, often after taking drugs, distressed; see also **zonked**. Also **out there** (1) *out of control* 'too high' (2) *mentally ill*

out of time *too late to appeal* unless a court gives leave

Outreach Christian programme working with prisoners and taking them to speak in churches etc. in the local community

overnight *overnight pass*

overs *surpluses* profits from crime not yet divided out among a gang or group of offenders

over the fence, over the hill, over the wall *escaped, on the run:* see **away**

P

PA prison auxillary who may help in the **canteen,** distribute newspapers and mail, book visits etc

PAC *Penal Affairs Consortium* umbrella organization for 31 other groups involved in the criminal justice process. Publishes papers on criminal justice topics (including sentencing) and makes representations to Parliament and others

PACE *Police and Criminal Evidence Act 1984* the statute which governs police interviews with suspects, police detention of suspects and related items

pack of three *condoms* packet of three

pad *cell* possibly from padlock; can be used to mean **padded cell:** see generally **cell.** Also: **pad clean** clean your own cell; see also **slop out; pad mate** prisoner with whom a cell is shared; **pad shark** prisoner who steals from cells; see also **Peter thief, Peter thin**

paddy wagon *prison transport* 'may derived from the significant number of people of Irish descent (i.e. called 'Paddy') working in US police forces and prisons, or from padlock, or padded cell: see **Black Maria**

PAIN *Prisoners' Advice and Information Network* national umbrella organization incorporating **PROP, Inquest** and **Women in Prison**

palm oil *a bribe* to 'grease someone's palm': see **backhander**

panda/panda car *police car* i.e. black and white like a panda; see also **black and white, jam sandwich, Q boat**

P and P *pay and privileges* which can be taken away for disciplinary reasons at an **adjudication:** see also **privs**

panic button *alarm button* in prison interview/private visit room

pansy *effeminate/homosexual man:* see **bent**

paper *folded paper containing drugs:* see also **wrap**

84

paper dress/paper suit untearable garment worn by prisoners in **strip cells**; see also **space suit, strip dress, strips**

paper hanger someone who passes forged cheques; see also **kiter, laydown merchant, leafer, penman, scratcher, slinger**

papers *cigarette/drugs papers;* see also **leaves, Rizlas, skins, wafers**

PAR *parole assessment report* release under **DCR** partly depends on a PAR from the prison and the probation service

paraffin *dirty prisoner* (rhyming slang: *paraffin lamp = tramp*); see also **soap dodger**

parole *discretionary early release under supervision* the word **parole** is still in common use, but in fact, except for prisoners sentenced before 1 October 1992, there is no such thing as parole. The current system is called 'discretionary conditional release' (see **DCR**). The **Parole Board** still exists and makes recommendations for DCR. It operates mainly in relation to **DCR**; see also **lifers.** It comprises a chairman and around 80 members, of whom six are full time. It includes judges, psychiatrists, chief probation officers, criminologists and independent members. It meets in panels of three or four to consider cases, theoretically about eight weeks before a prisoner is due for release: see **ERP, parole.** Also **Parole Board review** the Parole Board reviews the sentences of people serving four years or more at intervals and may decide to recommend a move to a lower security category or open prison, or eventually to release the prisoner if it is satisfied he or she is no longer a risk to the public; **parole knockback** (**KB**) refusal to release someone; the prisoner is shown a **refusal paper** stating that release has been turned down; **parole window** the name given to the period between the parole eligibility date (**PED**) and the non-parole date (**NPD**). During this period some prisoners at first refused parole may be given a second chance.

parsley see **marijuana**

PAS see **Prisoners' Advice Service**

pass key prison keys: see **gate, spanners, thins, twirl**

Maryann

Pat down

pat down *body search* particularly by prison officers; see also **frisk, rub down**

85

patch *territory* of a gang, prostitute or drug dealer; area patrolled by police; see also **manor, turf**

patches *prisoner(s) thought likely to try to escape.* From the yellow patches on their jacket and trousers, which may also have yellow stripes; see also **away, book, Cat-A etc, E-list, E-man, patches, stripes, trotter, wallflower**

path lab *pathology laboratory* where **forensic** enquiries are carried out

patsy *scapegoat;* see also **fall guy**

Patsy Cline *line* i.e. a **snort** of cocaine: see **C** (rhyming slang). After the US country and western singer; see also **rails**

patter *words, slang* i.e. prison patter

pay enquiry when a prisoner asks about the amount of money he or she has earned

pay out/pay and out when a prisoner is released on payment of a fine where he or she has been committed to prison in default

PC *previous convictions;* see also **form, former, mileage, previous, record, sheet, yellow sheet**

PCO *prison custody officer* name used in 'private prisons' for a prison officer; see also **contracted prisons**

PCU *Prisoner Casework Unit* in some prisons to process requests and complaints; see also **confidential access, R and C**

PCCU *Psychiatric Criminal Care Unit;* see also **Fraggle Rock, hospital unit, Muppet House**

PD *pretty disgusting*

PDR *pre-discharge report;* see also **discharge, PAR**

PDS *Prison Disciplinary System* prison governors hear day-to-day charges against prisoners (see **adjudication**), but if they feel the offence goes beyond their powers, i.e. where there are serious allegations the police may be called in. The **Board of Visitors** no longer has any disciplinary powers

PED *parole eligibility date* the earliest date when a prisoner serving four years or more can be released on parole. The PED will vary depending on whether the prisoner was sentenced before October 1992, when the present provisions came into force, in which case it will fall one third of the way through the sentence. If however the prisoner was sentenced after September 1992, the PED falls half way through the sentence. But if parole is not granted, the prisoner will have to wait till three quarters of the way through the sentence and this is known as the non parole date (**NPD**), or automatic release date (**ARD**). Prisoners released before this will in any case remain under supervision until their **NPD**. There are various reasons why prisoners fail to become eligible for parole. They may have had too many reports of bad behaviour, breaking of prison rules. Or they may be considered unstable and therefore unready to adjust to life outside prison

peek, in the prisoner under observation; see also **pegged**

peeper *detective:* see **brains**

pegged under surveillance, being watched; see also **peek, in the**

PEI, PEIO, PEO *physical education instructor, instructing officer;* see also **Adidas, gym orderly.** Also **PESO** physical education senior officer

Penal Affairs Consortium see **PAC**

penguin *prison officer* (from black and white uniform): see **screw**

penman *forger* e.g. of counterfeit money; see also **kiter, laydown merchant, leafer, paperhanger, scratcher, slinger**

P E P *Personal Empowerment Programme* anti-addiction programme imported from the US and used in some UK prisons

perimeter outer wall, fence or bounds of a prison

personal kit *a prisoner's own clothes*

personal officer each prisoner is given a personal officer who has a duty to look after that prisoner's interests and shar work with the prison probation officer in relation to a sentence plan (in the case of prisoners serving 12 months or more), and put the prisoner forward for courses, education etc.

personal property *a prisoner's possessions;* see also **IP**

personal services *sexual services* prostitution

personnel carrier euphemistic term for secure prison transport: see **Black Maria**

perve *pervert* sex offender, child molester: see **animal**

PET *Prisoners' Education Trust* charity that helps fund prisoners who wish to study in prison or on release

peter (1) *cell* (from seventeenth century word *peter* meaning box or safe); see **cell**. (2) *bag of burglary tools* (3) *explosives,* i.e. saltpetre. Hence **peterman** = safebreaker

peter thin *prisoner who steals from cells* (regarded as the lowest of the low); also known as a **pad shark, peter thief**

petition *formal request* in writing to the governor (see also **app**) or even the Home Secretary

PFF *Prisoners' Families and Friends* national London-based advice and information service which can visit families of prisoners in the London area and offer advice, support and friendship

Phoenix Trust see **Prison Phoenix Trust**

phonecard deal e.g. when a prisoner swaps a prison **phonecard** for a **joint;** see also **deal, green and friendly, half-ounce deal**

photogenic, to *remember 'photographically'* i.e. used as a verb. 'I could photogenic the credit cards and keys'; see also **doing cards, on the plastic**

pie and chips *equal opportunities* used by women prisoners as a wry comment, i.e 'a man's diet/world'

piece of duff *homosexual rent boy*

piece of steel *knife 'home made' in jail;* see also **chiffy, shiv, stringer**

pigs *the police:* see **Bill**

pigsty *police station:* see **bill shop**

pill popper *addict* taking drugs in pill form; see also **downer, speedfreak**

pill pusher *doctor:* see also **scablifter, SMO, vet**

pillow biter *male homosexual:* see **bent** .

pills, power pills *Ecstasy:* see **E**

pinch minute amount of **marijuana**

pin down *form of restraint* used (or formerly used) on young people in secure units

pink cadillac *Ecstasy:* see **E**

pink champagne *amphetamines (speed)* in powder form: see **A**

pinned *using drugs* from pinsize pupils when using hard drugs: see **H**

pipe used for **crack** cocaine and other drugs

pips *'buttons' on the shoulders of prison officers' uniforms* denoting rank

pissed cell fashion *messing up a cell by pouring/spraying urine about* a **dirty protest**; see also **potting up, shitting up, shit shaped**

piss test *urine test* prisoners' usage; see also **MDT, taking the piss**

pit bulls *Ecstasy:* see **E**

placer person who places stolen goods with a **fence**; see also **buyer, handling, receiver**

plant *false evidence* i.e. to incriminate someone

plastic gangster *phoney tough guy*

plastics *prison knife, fork and spoon* made of plastic to prevent attacks or self-mutilation. Issued on **reception** into prison

plates *number plates* (e.g. false number plates on a stolen car)

playing bingo sex offender (from the **numbers** in **Rule 43**): see **animal**

playtime *free association* when prisoners are allowed out of their cells to mix with others; see **association, free-flow, full association, split association, Wendy house**

plead *plead innocent* reversal of the use of 'plead' within the official criminal justice process, where this is usually taken to mean 'plead guilty' unless expressly stated otherwise; compare **cop a plea**

plod *policeman* (from Mr. Plod the policeman in Enid Blyton's *Noddy* books): see **Bill**. Hence **plod shop** *police station;* see also **bill shop**

plonk *woman police officer*

PLP *Prison Link Project:* organization which gives confidential advice and support to prisoners about to be released. Contrast the organisation **Prison Link**

88

plugging putting drugs or other items in the anus during a visit to smuggle them into a prison: see **bottling, charger**

plunged *stabbed to death*

PMO *Principal Medical Officer* full-time doctor employed by Prison Medical Service; see also **pill pusher, SMO, vet**

PMS *Prison Medical Service* now renamed Health Care Service for Prisoners: see **HCSP**

PMU *population management unit* which deals with movement of prisoners

PNS *principal nursing sister*

PO (1) *probation officer* (2) *principal [prison] officer* (3) **personal officer**

POA *Prison Officers' Association*

pod *central kitchen* on some **wings**

POL 1 *exceptional risk* a police POL 1 form accompanies prisoners regarded as at high risk of suicide/serious self-harm coming into prison. They are meant to be kept under surveillance; see also **special watch, SSS**

politician see **jail politician**

ponce (1) *pimp* **ponce off** *live off immoral earnings* (a criminal offence) (2) **ponce about** *dress up, act stupidly/showily*

pontoon prison sentence of one year and nine months. From the card game in which a hand of 21 is 'a pontoon'

pony (1) *rubbish, crap, shit* (2) *£25*

poof, poofter *male homosexual:* see **bent**

pop (1) *an escape attempt:* see **away** (2) *take drugs* to 'pop pills'. Contrast **skin pop** *an injection* (3) *arrest:* see **nicked**

poppers *amyl nitrite;* see also **hardcore**

POPS *Partners of Prisoners and Families Support Group* Manchester-based organization that helps prisoners' families nation-wide, offering a wide range of information and support

pork scratches *matches* (rhyming slang). From pork scratchings, a savoury snack

porridge *sentence served in prison;* see also **bird, bit, cons, lagging, time**

pot see **marijuana**

pothead *a* **marijuana** *user*

pot A *potential **Cat A** prisoner* If a prisoner is sentenced to ten years or more he or she is regarded as a potential Cat A prisoner. Women prisoners are not so categorized: they are simply assigned to open or closed conditions

potting up *throwing urine or excrement around;* see also **dirty protest, on the blanket**

pound *five year sentence*

POUT *prison officer under training*

POW *prostitution outreach work*

powder drug which may be in powder form, e.g. cocaine (see **C**), amphetamines (see **A**), heroin (see **H**)

power pill *Ecstasy:* see **E**

power rangers see **LSD**. From the TV cartoon characters

pox *marijuana*

poxy *rotten, disgusting;* see also **PD**

PPA *prison parole assessment*

PP nined *assaulted* hit with a battery (usually concealed in a sock). A PP9 is a heavy, standard size electric battery. Also a play on 'assault and battery'.

PPRS *preferred planning reporting system*

PPRR *performance planning and review record*

PR *prison riot; see also **riot bell***

PRES *pre-release employment scheme* whereby certain prisoners are allowed to spend some time living in a hostel, house or flat before release, either inside or outside of prison

previous *previous conviction(s);* see also form, **former, mileage, PC, record, sheet, yellow sheet**

primitive allocation prison officer jargon for allocating prisoners to other prisons without much time to consider individual needs

prison bent/prison gay someone who takes part in homosexual or lesbian activity only while in prison; reverting to heterosexual behaviour on release

Prisons Act *Prisons Act 1952*

Prison Discipline Manual contains the Prison Rules. Prisoners are advised to consult it before an **adjudication** hearing. A copy should be available in each prison library

Prison Fellowship international volunteer-based Christian ministry to prisoners, ex-prisoners and their families, offering practical and spiritual support

Prison Link Birmingham based organization to help bridge the gap between Black and Asian prisoners and their families. Services include a pre-release scheme, befriending and counselling for prisoners' families, driving families to visits and a club for the children of prisoners

Prison Phoenix Trust group that supports prisoners in their spritual lives, teaches them meditation and encourages and trains accredited yoga and meditation teachers to teach in prisons all over the UK

prison number every sentenced prisoner is given a number on **reception** and this stays with him or her throughout the entire sentence, including moves from one prison to another

prison visitor *volunteer who visits prisoners* often those who would otherwise have no **visit**. 'Prison visitors' do not need a **VO**. Usually, **chaplain** organizes local people to take part. Also **prison visitor liaison officer** a designated individual appointed by the governor to promote visiting; see also **NAPV**

90

Prisoners' Advice Service
provides advice and information to
prisoners in England and Wales
regarding their rights, particularly
concerning the application ôf
Prison Rules. Takes up prisoners'
complaints about their treatment,
taking legal action where
appropriate. Does not deal with
appeals or alleged miscarriages of
justice

**Prisoner's Wives and Families
Society** national London-based
group run by and for prisoners'
families. Offers information and an
overnight stay hostel for families
visiting London or passing through
London on the way to a visit. Also
runs a holiday scheme for
prisoners' families

Prison Watch Network to support
prisoners and families, especially
those at risk of self harm or suicide.
Based in Bristol and Derby

privacy screens used especially
for strip searches and mandatory
drug testing (see **MDT**)

private spends, private cash
money sent into prison by relatives
ôr friends, or any (usually small)
amount of cash a prisoner is
carrying on **reception.** A certain
sum is allowed to prisoners each
week for small purchases from the
prison **canteen** for cigarettes, food,
phone cards, batteries, toiletries
etc. Prisoners used to be allowed
unlimited amounts of cash but since
the introduction of **IEPS** in 1995,
prisoners' cash depends on
whether they are on **Basic,**
Standard or **Enhanced** regimes.
Every new prisoner starts on
'standard rate', currently £10 private
cash which may be spent each
week, rising to £15 if on 'enhanced
rate' (prisoners of good behaviour,

who have never been on report).
The rate can drop to a basic of
£2.50 if prisoners refuse to go to
work or are on report for bad
behaviour. This can be
supplemented by wages earned for
work in prison, which are low
compared with work outside prison:
even the highest rates amount to
less than £20 a week. Different
rules apply to **unconvicted
prisoners** (All figures as at 1996)

privatisation scheme whereby
prisons are run by private
contractors rather than the state. As
of 1996, the privately run prisons
are HMPs Blakenhurst, Doncaster,
The Wolds and Buckley Hall; see
also **contracted prisons, PCO**

privileges anything allowed to
prisoners which they cannot have
as of right. Loss of privileges, such
as **association,** tobacco, radio is a
common punishment at an
adjudication; see also **privs**

privileged wing wing in a prison
where prisoners of good behaviour
are housed. They are usually those
on an **Enhanced** regime; see **IEPS**

privs see **privileges**

prob/probation most prisons have
in-house probation officers
seconded by the local probation
service and paid for out of the
prison governor's budget, though
their numbers are being trimmed in
response to tighter prison budgets

probation box prisoners have to
make an **app** (application) to see a
probation officer and this can be put
in the probation box

production prison officer jargon for
when a prisoner appears in court. A
prison production is the process

whereby a prisoner is brought to court by prison officers, rather than by, e.g. **Group Four**

PROP national prisoners' movement, formerly called 'Preservation of the Rights of Prisoners'. Ex-prisoner organization set up in 1972. Handles enquiries from prisoners and their families from an ex-prisoner standpoint and provides legal and medical back-up in cases of complaints about prison treatment

prop box *box for prisoners' own property/valuables* Kept in the **prop room**. Prison regulations have been tightened up concerning the amount of property allowed in cells. In some prisons this has been reduced to what will fit in two prop boxes plus one outsize object, partly to facilitate faster cell searches. All prisoners are normally allowed to keep some personal possessions at the governor's discretion, e.g. a radio, wristwatch, book, pen and paper; see also **IP, two box system, volumetrics.** Also **prop card** property card on which a prisoner's property is listed on his or her **reception** into prison; see also **disclaimer form**

protected room ultimate provision in a prison health care centre where a prisoner is held for his or her own protection. Only the prison doctor can make the order for the prisoner to be so held; see also **block, 1980 cell, strip cell, unfurnished room**

PRR *post-recall release* a prisoner released early can be recalled. After returning to complete more of the original sentence, he or she can be re-released on PRR

PRS *Prisoners' Resource Service* specialist non-statutory sector

organization providing advice, support and referral services to prisoners in the South East of England who have concerns about drugs, alcohol or HIV/AIDS

PRT *Prison Reform Trust* national charity that campaigns for better conditions in prison and the greater use of alternatives to custody. Deals with individual enquiries and complaints about treatment in prison, runs a prisoners' penfriend scheme. Publishes a quarterly newsletter called *Prison Report* and other information about prisons

PSDS *Prison Service Drug Strategy*

PSIF *Prison Service Industries and Farming*

PSR *pre-sentence report* (used to be called **social inquiry report** (SIR)). Prepared by a probation officer (in the case of young offenders this may be a social worker) in accordance with a National Standard for Pre-sentence Reports. A PSR is used to assist courts in deciding on a suitable way of dealing with an offender. The PSR includes an analysis of the current offence and the circumstances leading up to it; relevant information about the offender including previous patterns of offending; an assessment of risk to the public of reoffending by the offender; and information on any suitable community sentence

PT *part-time*

PTE *part-time education*

puff (1) from *poof = homosexual man:* see **bent.** (2) *smoke* **marijuana**

92

pull *stop and search/arrest* **pulled** *arrested;* see also **nicked, sus**

pull time, to *to be put in prison*

punter (1) *prostitute's client* (2) loose way of describing almost any customer or potential victim of a property offence

pup, buy a *to be the victim of swindling*

purple gnomes see **LSD**

purple haze see **marijuana**

purple hearts *amphetamines (speed)* in the shape of a purple heart (a term also associated with a US forces medal): see **A**

push *sell drugs* **pusher** *drug seller*

push in *rob someone on their doorstep*

pussy drunk *sex offender:* see **animal**

put one together *plan a crime*

put the block on *enforce stricter regulations*

put the name in the hat *inform:* see **grass**

put the sleeve on *arrest;* see also **nicked**

put your hands up *plead guilty* i.e. 'surrender'

PV (1) *parole violator* prisoner who breaks conditions of parole. (2) *prison visitor*

PVM *Prisons Video Magazine* bi-monthly video programme issued within the prison system with a view to promoting understanding and sharing good practice among all involved in the prison community. Has been running since 1991

PVO *privileged visiting order* = extra **VO**, only allowed on certain days. Each prison has different rules, e.g. one women's prison offers two extra VOs every 28 days. These are **PVOs** which may only be used on Tuesdays and Thursdays. They may not be saved up as VOs can be, and are void if not used up in time. They must be used within 28 days and cannot be re-issued or transferred. Prisoners on **Enhanced** regimes are allowed PVOs as a privilege, pursuant to **IEPS.** PVOs can occasionally be granted if a prisoner is seriously ill, or has grave family problems, or, in the case of foreign nationals, if relatives have travelled from overseas and are only in the country for a few days; see also **enhanced visit, differential regimes, VO**

Q

qat, qaadka, khat *green leaf of the shrub Catha edulis* a narcotic, halucinogenic, stimulant chewed across East Africa. Seemingly, not unlawful in the UK

Q boat *police car* (unmarked); see also **black and white, jam sandwich, panda**

QE *turn Queen's evidence* Give evidence for the prosecution, usually against alleged accomplices in return for improved treatment, credit in relation to the level of the charges brought against the person turning QE or in relation to sentence

quarter *quarter of a kilo of drugs;* also known as a **quarter of a K/key** (2) *quarter of an ounce of cocaine:* see generally **C**

Queen, for the extra days on sentence: 'I had to do five days extra for the Queen', i.e. five **ADAs**

queen *homosexual man, usually ageing;* see also **closet queen**

queer *homosexual man:* see also **bent**

queer-bashing *attacking male homosexuals* usually by a gang of youths, as if for sport

quill *heroin:* see **H**

R

R and C *request and complaint* form which prisoners wishing to make a formal request or complaint must complete. The process may begin with a verbal communication to an officer, followed by an application to see the governor (see **app**), then if necessary a written formal request or complaint. If the prisoner remains dissatisfied he/she can appeal to the **area manager** and eventually to the **Prisons Ombudsman** and/or the **Board of Visitors;** see also **reserved subjects, confidential access**

R and R *rape and robbery*

rabbit *talk a lot* (rhyming slang: *rabbit and pork = talk*)

rad *radio* there are strict rules about the kind of radio prisoners can have. It must be battery-operated with no external lead (except in rare situations). It must only be able to receive long wave, medium wave,

short wave and FM frequencies; it cannot have an aerial with a long wire. There is also a size restriction at some prisons; see also **Brixton briefcase, ghetto blaster, rambler, sounds, talking handbag**

ragga *West Indian rap music*

raggas *young black men* usually meaning in a group or gang

rails *lines of cocaine:* see **C**. From the practice of using a razor blade to divide cocaine powder in thin lines on a mirror or glass; see also **line, Patsy Cline**

rake-off *profit* often excessive and illegal

rambler *radio;* see also **Brixton briefcase, ghetto blaster, rad, sounds, talking handbag**

rambo *prison officer 'with attitude'* From the US tough guy film character 'Rambo'; see **screw**

rap *charge, allegation* (derived from US slang). Hence **beat the rap** *to be acquitted*

RAPT *Rehabilitation for Addicted Prisoners Trust* (formerly called **ADT** = Addictive Diseases Trust). Charity that runs addiction treatment programmes in some prisons. RAPT opened its third drug and alcohol unit at HMP Pentonville in 1996

rap sheet a **record** of *previous convictions;* see also **former, mileage, PC, previous, yellow sheets**

rat *bad character*

rat on *inform on:* see **grass**

94

raver *male homosexual:* see **bent**

raving needle something that drives you mad: 'His constant music gives me the raving needle!'

razoring *cutting someone with a razor;* see also **cut up, scratcher, slasher, slicer**

RC *remand centre*

read the riot act explain legal restrictions concerning firearms to a prisoner before release

reader *book, magazine*

ready *ready money* money that can be used immediately

ready eye *police trap*

recall/recalled a prisoner released **on licence** may be recalled to prison if conditions are breached; see generally **AUR, ACR, DCR**

receive in property which a prison allows visitors to bring in for prisoners' use

receiving officer officer on duty to take in goods brought in for prisoners; see also **visit**

receiver (1) *prison that receives prisoners from other establishments* (2) *receiver of stolen property;* see also **fence, handling, placer**

reception (1) *reception area* where a prisoner is first received into prison. (2) the process of reception. Prisoners are usually taken to a **local prison** or **remand centre** from the court, generally in the early evening. They will be told to shower and will be given clothes (though female prisoners and remand prisoners can keep their own clothes). They are given a meal, a **prison number** (if sentenced) and a brief medical interview before being taken on to the wing. They may be photographed and fingerprinted. They are given a towel, sheets, and washing requisites, toothbrush etc. They may also receive an **advance** on their wages or, if they have come from another prison, until their money is transferred. They may also get an advance of tobacco and a **phonecard.** The following morning, new prisoners go for a **reception interview** before a **reception board** (usually consisting of a **principal officer** and another officer and sometimes a prison **probation officer**) where they are asked questions about their personal circumstances and their offence, and, if already sentenced, told their expected date of release (see **EDR**). Men will also be given a security category. All prisoners go before an **allocation board** and will be told whether or not they are to be transferred elsewhere. They also have a chance to see the **chaplain**. Also: **reception call** every new prisoner is allowed one free telephone call (usually after 6 p.m. when calls are less expensive); **reception letter** every new prisoner is allowed one letter to be sent second class, free of charge; **reception VO** new prisoners are given their first visiting order (**VO**) when they come into prison

recess washing area and toilets on wing (when **slopping out** of chamber pots was still common, each landing had large open sinks where prisoners emptied their chamber pots each morning)

95

record *criminal record;* see also **form, former, previous, mileage, PC, rapsheet, yellow sheet**

red band *band worn by trusted prisoners* who may be allowed to go about within the prison unsupervised, e.g to take messages or serve refreshments at visiting time; see also **orderly, trusty**

red dragons see **LSD**

red hots *Ecstasy:* see **E**

red letter *letter sent out illicitly via visitors* may contain information that prison authorities might object to, money from unlawful deals or illicit information; see also **stiff**

red rush *amyl nitrite:* see **hardcore**

red seal *cannabis:* see **marijuana**

reducing script *diminishing prescription for drug substitute* e.g. **Methadone.** Reducing amounts are prescribed, to enable prisoners to withdraw from addiction with fewer withdrawal symptoms. Not all prisons allow this method; see also **hit the doctor, juice, meth, script, three day chop**

reefer *dope cigarette:* see **bif, marijuana**

refusal paper document telling a prisoner that parole has been refused; see also **KB, knockback, parole knockback**

regime (1) **Basic, Standard** and **Enhanced:** see under those items. (2) system whereby a prison keeps its prisoners 'occupied in purposeful work'. A **regimes manager** is given the job of organizing regime activities. (3) More generally, the term is used by courts and officials to mean the overall regime or regimes in prisons or in a given establishment

regs regulations, rules of prison: see **Rules**

rehab/rehabilitation *programme, unit for addicts recovering from drug or alcohol dependency*

rehabilitation period a conviction is regarded as legally 'spent' when a fixed period has expired from the date of the conviction. After this period. with certain exceptions, the ex-offender is not normally obliged to mention the conviction when applying for a job or obtaining insurance. This does not apply to prison sentences of more than two and a half years. The length of the rehabilitation period depends on the length of the original sentence and the age of the prisoner, e.g. a **YO** aged less than 18 at conviction, serving six months or less, would be given a rehabilitation period of three and a half years, while a person over 18 serving the same sentence would have a longer period, seven years

remand when an accused person is in custody or on **bail** awaiting trial or sentence. **remand concessions** remand prisoners are presumed innocent unless later convicted and thus allowed certain concessions e.g. more cigarettes, unlimited spending money and a visit every day. **remand remission** time spent on remand counts against any custodial sentence imposed, but only once where consecutive sentences are given. This was the cause of corrective measures by the Home Secretary when, in 1996, it transpired that governors had been instructed to allow remand time against each such sentence and over 500 prisoners were wrongly released on that basis. The High Court confirmed that this was in error; see also **custody days**. Also **remand centre** prison, or section of a prison, where people remanded in custody are held pending trial or sentence

remedials *medical exercise*

remission apart from **lifers**, prisoners are released after serving part of their sentence: see **AUR, ACR, DCR**. The rest of the sentence is, in effect, remitted (now called **early release**). But they are subject to a combination of supervision, conditions and liability to **recall** to prison in certain situations. If prisoners break prison rules they can lose remission: see **ADAs**. They will then spend extra days in prison before release unless they win this **time back**; compare **remand remission**

rent boy *young male prostitute*

rep *reputation*

report sick *see the prison doctor;* see also hit the **doctor, vet**

reporting officer whose job it is to write reports on a prisoner's progress

reppoc *policeman* (backslang = *copper*) see: **Bill**

request see **R and C**

reserved subjects certain **R and C** matters can only be dealt with by the **area manager** or staff in Prison Service Headquarters

resettlement licence a form of release on **temporary licence** to

maintain family and community ties and make arrangements for accommodation, work and training when released; see also **RLED** *resettlement licence eligibility date* **resettlement prison** which specifically prepares prisoners at the end of their sentences for release into the community

resin *cannabis* see: **marijuana**

resi-pack a pack of residual items that goes with a prisoner transferred from one prison to another, such as records of visits, **adjudications**, applications (see **app**), in fact any current information

restoration of remission see: **time back**

restraints straps or chains used to restrain prisoners thought to be violent; male prisoners are restrained in handcuffs and women in leather wrist straps. A body belt may be used if necessary; see **ankle straps, bracelets, C and R, closeting chain, cross-cuffing, cuffs, shackles**

restricted regime when prisoners are held in isolated conditions for a limited period

restricted visit *closely supervised visit* allowed to a high security prisoner with special permission

result, to get a (1) get a favourable verdict in a trial or favourable answer to an application (see **app**) or request; see also **earner, squeeze.** (2) conversely when used by police or prosecutors, a successful prosecution

Riot bell

retainer list a prisoner going to court and wanting to keep his or her prison job or place on a training course can ask to be kept on the retainer list

retrievers *prisoners who intimidate or bully other prisoners* whom they suspect of carrying drugs; see also **searchers**

reversal doors cell doors usually open inwards, but because of increasing concern over prisoners barricading themselves in, and the danger of hostage taking, cells are being fitted with doors which can open outwards

review *check on a prisoner's progress*

rhubarb and custard *Ecstasy:* see **E**

rhubarbs see **LSD**

RIC (1) *remand in custody* (2) *rest in cell* when prisoner who is off work because of sickness is locked inside his or her cell. (3) euphemism for being **banged up**

ric *make a mistake*

ride it cope with being **banged up** in a cell/doing time in prison

right to the death, to go to wait until the start of a trial before taking a certain action, such as changing a plea from 'not guilty' to 'guilty'

right, to have a *buy physical protection*

rights, to be given to be informed about Prison **Rules** by an officer; compare **read the Riot Act**

rim *annilingus (homosexual slang)*

ringer (1) *double* e.g., 'He was a dead ringer for me' = 'He looked like me'. May imply mistaken identity/alibi. (2) *stolen and disguised item* usually a car (originally from same process for racehorses and greyhounds): 'I got three years for ringing cars': see also **bastardized.** (3) *someone who steals cars resprays them and fits false plates*

riot bell *any bell* including an alarm bell. **riot gear** *body armour etc.* see: **C and R**

risk assessment all prisoners serving 12 months or more and young offenders have to be 'risk assessed' before being released on licence (see **ACR, DCR**) to see whether conditions should be added to the licence. This also applies to **temporary release** for **resettlement licence** purposes, work outside prison etc.

Rizlas *cigarette papers* also used for **joints**. After the 'Rizla' brand name; see also **leaves, papers, skins, wafers**

RLED *resettlement licence eligibility date* **HLED** *home leave eligibility date* has been replaced by **RLED**; see also **PED**

roach, roche (1) *drug cigarette* often containing **marijuana** (derived from US slang). (2) *tab end* the 'hot' and thereby unpopular end of a cigarette: see **bif**

roasting *anxious, upset;* see also **gutted, screwing**

rock *lump of* **crack** *cocaine;* also pure small **cocaine** crystals (see **C**), heroin (see **H**); see also **on the rock, stone, wash**

rocky, rocky black see **marijuana**

rod *automatic gun* (derived from US slang); see also **gat, heater, shooter**

rogues' gallery *police collection of* **mugshots** i.e. head and shoulders photographs of criminals

roll *the number of prisoners in an establishment;* see also **average roll**

roll check *prisoner tally* following the opening of cell doors between 7.30 a.m. and 8 a.m. and locking up around 9 p.m. in the evening; see also **muster**

roll, to (1) *make a tobacco cigarette* **roll a joint** make a **marijuana** cigarette. (2) *rob/fleece a punter* including by a prostitute demanding prior payment then quitting the scene

roller *prostitute who makes off with the money* i.e. without providing sex; see also **clipper, clip joint**

roll-up *handrolled cigarette;* see also **bif**

rooftop demo *disturbance* when prisoners climb onto the roof to protest

rookie *new police officer* (possibly from 'recruit'); see also **choirboy**

room *cell* **room spin** *cell search;* see also **cell spin, spin, swoop, TO, twirl**

rope *vein* into which drugs are injected; see **mainline, tie off, tie up, tie off, tracks**

ro-ro *'roll on roll off' educational course* whereby, e.g. **short term** prisoners can complete individual modules: see also **NVQ**

rory *cell door* (rhyming slang: *Rory O'Moor = door*)

rose garden *solitary confinement* cell; see **block**

Rosie Lee (1) *prison tea* (rhyming slang); see also **cup of diesel**. (2) *prison flea* (rhyming slang): see also **loppy**

rough trade *homosexual prostitution*

rough up usually meaning to **mug**

route form *outside travel permit for prison staff*

rover *prison officer on duty patrolling the wing;* see also **hiker, ranger:** see generally **screw**

rower *row, argument;* see also **ruck**

Royal Mail see **bail** (rhyming slang)

rozzer *policeman* (possibly from the Romany *roozlo = strong*): see **Bill**

R R L O *Race Relations Liaison Officer* every prison is obliged to appoint such an officer whose job it is to help prisoners who feel they have been discriminated against and to make sure the laws on race relations are followed

RRMT *Race Relations Management Team* to monitor and investigate allegations of racial discrimination and make sure ethnic minority prisoners are given equal treatment to white prisoners. The **R R L O** *Race Relations Liaison Officer* and the **governor** must belong to the team

rub down prisoner is searched quickly by officers running hands over body; see also **frisk, pat down**

rubber cheque *cheque which will bounce;* see also **sturmer, lay a kite**

ruck *a fight or argument;* see also **rower**

Rules, the Prisons operate under various sets of Rules: those set out pursuant to the Prison Act 1952; those listed in Prison Rules 1964; and those in the Young Offender Institution Rules 1988. Some of the rules most commonly mentioned by prisoners are listed below

Rule 43, on rule 43 is one of the 1964 Rules dealing with control and restraint of prisoners. It enables a

prisoner to be removed from association with other prisoners, usually for the maintenance of good order and discipline (see **GOD, GOAD**). It means he or she is kept with other Rule 43 prisoners and/or in isolation. Many prisoners 'go on Rule 43' at their own request because they are in danger from other prisoners, usually due to nature of their offence, e.g child molesting, or because they are a police informer (see **grass**), or they may have been a police officer, prison officer etc, or they may be at risk because of their behaviour in prison, e.g. running up escalating debts to other prisoners. But the governor can put a disruptive prisoner on Rule 43 for the protection of other people. The maximum period of isolation is initially three days, then a member of the **BOV** has to be consulted and may extend the application of the rule to up to a month. It can then be reviewed and be renewed if necessary; see also **VP, VPU, Rule, Rule 46, Rule 47, numbers, numbered off**

Rule 46 equivalent of Rule 43 for GOAD as used in **YOIs** for prisoners under 21 years of age, when it can only be applied for a maximum of two weeks at a time

Rule 47 sets out the offences against prison discipline which can be summarized as follows:

1. assault 2. detaining another person 3. denying an officer access to part of the prison 4. fighting 5. intentionally endangering health of others 6. obstructing an officer 7. escaping/absconding 8. breaking rules of temporary release 9. possessing an unauthorised article 10. selling an article to another prisoner 11. selling one of his or her own possessions 12. taking another prisoner's belongings 13.

100

setting fire to the prison 14. destroying or damaging property 15. not being In the right place at the right time 16. being disrespectful to an officer or visitor 17. using abusive, threatening or insulting words/behaviour 18. refusing to work/work properly 19. disobeying orders 20. disobeying rules 21. offending against **GOAD** 22. commiting/inciting others to commit any of the 21 offences already set out. This rule also sets out the punishments that can be inflicted on a prisoner who commits any of the above offences

There are seven main punishments:

1. caution. 2. loss of privileges for up to 42 days 3. stopping wages for up to 42 days 4. confinement in cell for up to 14 days. 5. up to 42 extra days in prison 6. exclusion from work 7. (for unconvicted prisoners who escape or try to escape) loss of the right to wear own clothes

Rule 48 This rule deals with disciplinary charges: it demands that a prisoner must be charged with any such offence against prison discipline within 48 hours of offence being discovered. The prisoner is then kept segregated while offence is investigated

runner (1) *escaper see away* (2) *a prisoner dealer in tobacco or drugs* for the main **heads** or **barons** including collecting payments

rush (1) *amyl nitrite;* see **hardcore** (2) *instant intense effect of taking a drug*

Russian roulettes see **LSD**

RWV *robbery with violence*

S

sabbing *acting as a hunt saboteur*

sack *bag of heroin;* see also **boot, bagel, finger, joey, scorebag, paper, wrap**

safe screw *corrupt prison officer;* see **screw, bent screw**

sagging, sagging off *truanting from work/school*

saint *incorruptible* i.e. police office or prison officer

salami fraud *'creaming off' fraud* in which investors' profits/interest are 'sliced off' and paid into fraudster's own account

salmon *tobacco* (rhyming slang: *salmon and trout = snout*); see also **burn.** Usually implying a superior brand of cigarettes (especially Benson & Hedges): see **bif**

SAO *serious arrestable offence*

SASU *Suicide Awareness Support Unit*

saucers *Ecstasy:* see **E**

sawn-off *sawn off shotgun*

scablifter *doctor:* see **pill pusher, SMO, vet**

scag, skag *heroin* (derived from US slang): see **H**. Also **scaghead** *heroin addict;* see also **baghead, smackhead, smack freak**

scalp *ticket tout*

scam *large scale swindle* fraud, usually involving a business front; see also **skank**

scared shitless *extremely frightened;* see also **brick it, shitting bricks**

scared straight US method of tackling offending by bringing young offenders into prisons

Scoobie, Scoobie-doo *prison officer* (rhyming slang = *screw*): see **screw.** Scoobie-doo is a children's TV cartoon character

scoobied *messed around by a prison officer* (from **Scoobie-doo**); see also **fuck off merchant**

score (1) *buy drugs* (2) *profit from crime* (3) *get a result:* see also **earner.** (4) *acquire something* in prison (5) *£20*

scorebag *£20 worth of drugs;* see also **bag, finger, joey, paper, wrap**

scorpions *Ecstasy:* see **E**

scran (1) *informer* (backslang for narc): see **grass** (2) *prison food:* see **cob, cobitis, muck truck**

scratch *money*

scratch for work when police are keen to make an arrest

scratcher (1) *counterfeiter* usually of banknotes. (2) *safety match* prisoners are not always allowed matches; see also **clipper** (3) *self-mutilator;* see also **cutter, razoring, slasher, slicer**

scream *inform:* see **grass.** Also **screamer** (1) *informer* (2) *homosexual;* see **bent.**

screw (1) *prison officer* from the turning of the screw on the metal box outside a cell door to make it

more difficult for the prisoner within to turn a handle which caused a mechanism to grind small stones into dust. Alternatively from thrumbscrew: see the Introduction, pp.11-12. Other common names include:

> **boss, caser, cloddy, discipline officer, Dr Who, flue, four be two, fuck off merchant, German, jailee, jailer, kanga(roo), key, hiker, Mr. Busy, nick 'em and stick 'em, night ranger, penguin, PO, Rambo, ranger, rover, saint, Scoobie-doo, shitparcel, tube, turnkey, twirl, uniform, whiteshirt**

(2) *housebreak* (3) *fleece*

screwdriver *principal officer;* see also **SO, whiteshirt**

screwing (1) *anxious, upset* 'Leave me alone, I'm screwing!'; see also **gutted, roasting** (2) *housebreaking*

script (1) *letter* (2) *drugs prescription;* see also **hit the doctor, reducing script**

Scrubs, The *HMP Wormwood Scrubs,* West London

SCS *Serious Crime Squad*

scum *sex offender:* see **animal**

searchers prisoners who intimidate or bully other prisoners they suspect of carrying drugs; see also **retrievers**

second storey man *cat burglar;* see also **dancer, high wall job**

secs *Seconal* a barbiturate sleeping drug misused by addicts; see also **barb, barbs**

Section criminal offences are often referred to by the section of the Act

102

under which the prisoner was charged, e.g. 'I was nicked under section 12 (**twocking**) and section 22 (**handling** stolen property)' (in those instances sections of the Theft Act 1968). Other sections commonly referred to are those in the Offences Against the Person Act 1861: section 18 (**GBH**), section 20 (malicious wounding), section 38 (resisting arrest), section 47 (**ABH**)

Section 53 a provision of the Children and Young Persons Act 1933 which allows for the detention of certain young offenders for longer than two years: see also **Her Majesty's pleasure**

secure training centre for 12-14 year olds inclusive: five are planned nation-wide (1996)

SED *sentence expiry date* even when a prisoner is released early (see **AUR, ACR, DCR**), he or she is still liable for recall until the **SED** has passed

see ya round like a Polo *goodbye*

seg *segregation:* see **block**

sell-out *on the side of the authorities* or perceived to be so; see also **bounty, coconut**

send down when the judge sends an offender to prison (in some instances 'down the steps' to the cells below the courtroom)

sent to ghost town *transferred to another prison without warning;* see also **ghosted, on the ghost train, shanghaied, shipped out, skulldragged**

sentence planning system whereby in consultation with prison officers/probation officers prisoners plan their sentence to make sure they make the best use of their time in custody; at present, sentence planning applies only to prisoners with sentences of 12 months or more, and to all young offenders; see also **career**

servery *where meals are served;* see also **hotplate, hotplate hamster, pod**

Shit & a Shave.

setup man *criminal who plans a crime*

sex case *sex offender:* see **animal**

SGO *sports and games officer;* compare **Adidas**

shackles popular name for a **closeting chain**, a chain about ten feet long, attached by handcuffs at one end to a prisoner, at the other to an officer, officially to enable the prisoner some degree of movement

103

and, e.g. to use the WC in privacy. This is used if a prisoner felt to be at risk of escaping leaves the prison, e.g. for court, hospital etc.

shanghaied *transferred to another prison without warning;* see also **ghosted, on the ghost train, sent to ghost town, ship, shipped out**

shared misery method of allocating duties and tasks to officers so that unsocial hours are shared out **shared misery circuit** *moving difficult prisoners around:* see **magic roundabout, twenty-eight day lie down**

sheet *record of previous convictions;* see also **former, mileage, PC, previous, yellow sheet**

shicer, shyster *cheat,* e.g. a crooked lawyer

shife *stab* 'shift' someone by stabbing; see **also shiv, shivvie**

shift *move prisons* 'I shifted around a lot'; see also **ghosted, magic roundabout, shanghaied, ship, shipped out, twenty-eight day lie down**

ship, shipped out, shipped off moved from one prison to another, often without warning; prisoners may be woken very early in the morning and given ten minutes to pack all their belongings into a large prison issue plastic bag ready for transfer to another prison. Officially the prison is supposed to tell prisoners when they are being moved but have the right to withold this information if it is felt there is a security risk. Officers commonly come into a cell and shout 'On the ship!'; see also **ghosted, on the ghost train, sent to ghost town, shanghaied, skulldragged**

shirt lifter *male homosexual:* see **bent**

shit *heroin:* see **H**. 'Shit' can refer to other drugs (e.g **crack** cocaine). 'I was **licking shit**'; see also **white shit** *cocaine* **shit and a shave** *short term of imprisonment;* see also bed and **breakfast, haircut**. Also **shitparcel** *prison officer:* see **screw; shit shover** *male homosexual:* see **bent; shitter** *burglar who defecates at the scene*

shitting bricks extremely scared; see also **brick it, scared shitless**

shitting up/shit shaped a **dirty protest** when a prisoner uses excrement or urine to daub the walls and sometimes to attack prison officers. First publicly associated with prisons in the H blocks holding IRA prisoners at the Maze prison, Northern Ireland

shiv, shivvie *weapon* made in jail out of sharpened rod with a cloth covered handle; see also **chiffy, piece of steel, shife, striper**. Also used as a verb i.e. *to stab with a shiv*

shooter *gun;* see also **gat, heater, rod**

shooting gallery *place where drug addicts customarily 'shoot up'* (inject drugs) and commonly share needles (thereby increasing the risk of contamination, poisoning, infection, transmitted diseases)

shoot up *inject drugs* especially heroin (see **H**); see also **bang, dig, fire up, fix, hit, jump**

shop *inform:* see **grass**

104

short prisoner almost at the end of his or her sentence

short con *minor confidence trick* Compare **big con, LF, scam**

short term traditionally, a prisoner serving up to 18 months. However, the Criminal Justice Act 1991 defined a short term prisoner as one serving under four years; see also **long term**

shot *injection,* dose of drugs; see also **bang, dig, fire up, fix, hit, jimmy**

shove shit uphill *anal intercourse*

shrooms see: **magic mushrooms**

shut down when all prisoners are locked in their cells, e.g. because of security alert or staff shortages; see also **bang up, lock up**

sin bin punishment **block**; see also **CC, cardboard city, chokey, seg**

sing (1) *confess* (2) *inform* In both cases implying substantial activity, as in 'sing like a canary': see generally **grass**

six and four *heroin* heavily cut with other substances: see generally **H**

skag, scag heroin: see **H.** Also **skaghead** heroin addict; see also **baghead, smackhead, smack freak**

skank *rip-off;* see also **clipper, LF, roll, scam**

skid artist *getaway car driver;* see also **just in caser, stoppo driver, wheel man**

skid row cell used for prisoners who cause a lot of trouble: see **block, strip cell**

skids *underpants;* see also **bills**

skin pop *inject drugs under the skin* not into a vein. Contrast **mainline, tie off, tie up**

skins *cigarette papers* Also used for rolling drug cigarettes; see also **leaves, papers, Rizlas, wafers**

skint *out of money;* see also **brassic**

skip *jump bail*

skipper *derelict property* where homeless sleep **skippering** *living rough*

skip rats *litter pickers;* see also **wombling**

skulldragged *pulled out of bed at crack of dawn* to be taken to another prison; see **shipped out, ghosted, on the ghost train**

skunk see **marijuana**

sky pilot *prison* **chaplain** also general usage, as in the *poem Our Padre* by John Betjeman

SL *special letter* which a prisoner is permitted to write to a professional such as his or her legal adviser. If the prisoner has no **private spends** the prison will pay for a first class stamp; see also **legal letter, OL**

slammer *prison* (derived from US slang): see **clink**

slash *urinate*

slasher *self-mutilator* usually cutting forearms with a razor or

105

broken glass; see also **cutter, razoring, scratcher, slicer**

slate see **marijuana**

sleepers *sleeping pills* also used illicitly as drugs; see also **mandies, secs, tems, tunes**

slicer/slicing *self-mutilation* usually by cutting the forearms with a razor or with broken glass; see also **cutting up, razoring, scratcher, slasher**

slinger *confidence trickster* who passes forged banknotes; see also **laydown merchant, leafer, paperhanger, penman, scratcher**

slip the cuffs *extricate from handcuffs* and escape: see **away**

slop out, slop time (1) *removing and cleaning food plates and bowls from a cell* (2) *mealtime;* see also **nosh, muck truck, trolley route** (3) before in-cell sanitation or night access to a W.C., emptying urine, excrement in the **recess**

slush *forged money*

slush fund *money for prisoner's family* while he or she is in prison, funded by associates

smack *heroin* maybe from the German *schmecken = to taste*; or from the 'kick' effect of the drug: see **H**. Also **smackhead, smack freak** *heroin addict;* see also **baghead, skaghead.** Also **smacked out** *high on heroin*

smacks *blows* in a fight; see also **taps**

smashed *drunk* or *high on drugs*

SMC *substance misuse co-ordinator* the individual appointed to implement a prison's anti-drugs strategy

smileys see **LSD**; from the smiling face logo on certain **tabs**

SMO *senior medical officer;* see also **scablifter, pill pusher, vet**

smoke see **bif, marijuana**

smokey see **block**

smoking usually means smoking dope (see **marijuana**)

smoking gun *incontrovertible evidence* (derived from US slang)

smudge *pornographic magazine(s)*

snake *informer* (from 'snake in the grass'): see **grass**

snatch *kidnap*

sneak job *housebreaking; see also* **screw/screwing**

sneezed (1) *arrested:* see **nicked** (2) *kidnapped*

sneeze out *confess ;* see also come **clean, cough, sing**

snide *informer:* see **grass**

sniff *inhale drugs*

snitch *informer:* see **grass**

snooter *addict who sniffs narcotics*

snort *sniff, inhale drugs* especially cocaine (see **C**)

snout (1) *tobacco* from practice when smoking was forbidden and prisoner would cup his hands over

106

his nose as if scratching, to hide his cigarette; see also **baccy, burn** (2) *informer:* see **grass**

snout baron *gang leader* in drug or tobacco dealing

snow *cocaine;* see **C**

snowballs *Ecstasy:* see **E**

snow bird *cocaine addict;* see also **cokehead, coke freak**

snowhearts *Ecstasy:* see **E**

SNS *senior nursing sister*

snuff movie film, usually sexually pornographic, in which a real person is killed as part of the action

S O (1)*senior officer;* see also **screwdriver, whiteshirt** (2) *standing order* standing orders guide prison governors and their staffs in enforcing and interpreting Prison **Rules**

soap (1) *a bribe:* see **backhander** (2) see **marijuana**. Also **soap bar** *block of* **cannabis.**Also **soap dodger** *prisoner who avoids washing;* see also **paraffin; soapy** *dirty, messy*

Social, the *Social Security* i.e. (1) any benefit agency. (2) state benefits

sonics see **LSD**. From the children's cartoon character *Sonic the Hedgehog*

sorrowful tale *three months in jail* (rhyming slang): see **carpet**

sorted (1) *beaten up* by other prisoners; see also **done** (2) *enough drugs for the moment*

SOTP *Sex Offender Treatment Programme* a nation-wide Prison Service initiative

sounds radio; see also **Brixton briefcase, ghetto blaster, rad, rambler, talking handbag**

Southall Black Sisters organization to help women, especially black women, in prison

SOVA *Society of Voluntary Associates* London based organization that recruits, trains and places volunteers to help prisoners and ex-prisoners

SP/having the SP *the lowdown* having key information. Short for 'starting price/position' (racing jargon); see also **clue up, give someone the office**

space suit *untearable pyjamas* issued to be worn in a **strip cell;** see also **paper dress, strip dress**

spaced out *effect of taking drugs* usually hallucinogenic. **spacy** under the effects of drug

Spanish fly *aphrodisiac* costs £20 a bottle from sex shops (1996). Intended for mating bulls

spanners *prison keys;* see also **pass key, thins, twirl**

SPAR *staff planning and reporting system*

sparked *knocked out*

Special K *Ketamine* a drug in tablet form which produces hallucinations. A sedative used as an anaesthetic

special cell euphemism for a cell in the segregation/punishment **block;** see **block, CC, chokey, seg**

special diets prisoners may request special food for religious or medical reasons, e.g. vegetarian, vegan, Halal for Muslims, Kosher for Jews, and rice-based diets; see also **OD**

special letters see **SL**

special (1) *special psychiatric hospital* e.g. Broadmoor, Rampton, Ashworth. (2) *special constable* (3) Northern Ireland usage for certain police, courts

special sick prisoners who are ill after 4.30 p.m. must 'report to special sick' and a nurse should attend to them before they are locked in their cells

special visits if a prisoner is ill or has a serious family crisis or very important business to deal with, he or she can apply (see **app**) for an extra visit

special watch *watch on high risk prisoners* (those likely to escape, self-mutilate or commit suicide). Officers should look into the cell at least every 15 minutes; see also **POL 1, SSS, suicide watch**

specking *wandering around looking for houses to burgle 'on spec'* i.e. easy targets; see also **in and out man, lightfoot**

speed *amphetamines:* see **A,** Speed is *the* common alternative name for amphetamines

speedballing *mixing heroin and cocaine;* see also **H and C.** See generally **C** and **H.**

speedfreak *amphetamines* (see **A**) *addict;* see also **downer, pill popper.**

spell *three month jail sentence:* see **carpet**

speng *stupid:* see **bagel**

spent conviction a conviction which should not normally be mentioned and is legally regarded as spent: see the outline under the heading **rehabilitation period**

spiel *illicit gambling racket*

spike (1) *syringe* for injecting drugs; see also **hypo** (2) *add* a drug (e.g. Ecstasy: see **E**) or alcohol to a drink

spill the beans *inform:* see **grass**

spin *search premises unexpectedly;* see also **cell spin, TO, twirled**

spin a drum *search a house before a burglary;* see also **drum, drummer, swoop**

spin, room-spin *search a prison cell or other room unexpectedly;* see also **cell spin, TO, twirled**

spiv *blackmarket operative*

spliff, to spliff *smoke a **marijuana** cigarette;* see also **bif**

split association there are times when, usually due to staff shortage, only half of the prisoners on a **wing** can be let out for **association** at any one time

SPO *senior probation officer*

spook *spy*

spoon *measure of heroin:* see **H**

spray *aerosol for sniffing solvents;* see also **glue, nosebag, stickup**

spring, to *help a prisoner escape*

spur *group of cells* on a prison wing or **landing**

Squad, the the **flying squad** (usually meaning Scotland Yard or Regional Crime Squad detectives, or those from the proposed National Crime Squad (1996)); see also **lying squad, Sweeney**

square box *witness box* i.e. in a court

squat team *swoop team* (especially at HMP Holloway): see that item

squeal/squealer *inform/informer:* see **grass**

squeeze (1) *a light sentence* (2) *a request* or *application* (see **app, R and C**) which turns out in a prisoner's favour, e.g. the result of an appeal or governor's adjudication; see also **earner, result**

squidgy black see **marijuana**

S S *suspended sentence* i.e. of imprisonment Also known as a **bender**

SSCU *Segregation Security and Care Unit*

SSS *strict suicide supervision* prisoners felt to be at risk are issued with a form called the Self-harm at Risk Form and have to be closely supervised. Each prison is meant to have a suicide awareness team; see also **bed watch, POL I, special watch, suicide watch**

Ssss . . . *informer* (from hissing sound of a snake in the grass): see **grass**

stage rooms *recreation rooms* in prison; see also **association**

stand up *refuse to confess, cooperate when interrogated*

Standard regime the average regime, under which the majority of prisoners are held. Below that is **Basic,** without any privileges. Above it is **Enhanced,** with extra privileges like additional visits and more private cash being allowed. The three regimes are used as incentives or punishments; see **differential regimes, IEPS**

star (1) prisoner serving first custodial offence; see also **first bird, fish, new fish;** compare **starred up** (2) see **LSD**

stardust *cocaine* (derived from US drugs slang): see **C**

starred up when a young offender turns 21 and moves to an adult prison; see also **YP.** Compare **star**

stash (1) *hidden loot* (stolen goods, money, drugs): originally from the combination of **store** and **cash.** (2) *concealed drugs,* e.g. a small pack of **smack** wrapped in foil or clingfilm and hidden inside the mouth. **stash, to make for a** *steal drugs from another addict*

stay safe same as **take care** and **keep your head down:** all common ways of ending letters by prisoners

steamer *punter* old fashioned term but now in vogue with the young

steaming when a gang of muggers run through crowds of people robbing them

steps, up the *on trial;* see also **up the stairs**

sterile area *area immediately inside the perimeter wall of a prison* **Reception** and **admin** are in this area

stickup *glue for sniffing;* see also **glue, nosebag, spray**

stiff (1) *letter illicitly passed to visitors* which usually contains information that the authorities might object to, illegal information or money from drug dealing; see also **red letter** (2) *dead body*

sting *overcharge, cheat;* see also **big con, roll, clip joint, short con**

stir *prison* (maybe from the Romany *stariben,* which means *to confine*); see also **away, inside, jugged, in jug, in the nick.** Also **stir crazy, stir happy** *mad after a period in prison*

stick *riot baton*

stitch up *incriminate* usually by planting false evidence; see also **set up**

stone see **crack**

stoned *effect of taking alcohol or (usually soft) drugs*

stoolie *informer* (from **s t o o l pigeon:** a pigeon tied to a stool to act as a decoy): see **grass**

stoppo driver *getaway car driver;* see also **just in caser, skid artist, wheelman**

straight (1) *heterosexual* (2) *off drugs;* see also **clean**

straight, to go *to stop committing criminal offences;* also to **go on the straight and narrow**

straight down the line *honestly* 'I told them straight down the line. I had nothing to do with it.'

straight goer *someone not at all involved in criminal activities*

straightened *corrupted*

straightener *fight*

strap *interrogate harshly;* see also **third degree**

strapped *short of money* strapped for cash; see also **brassic**

straps prisoners thought to be violent are sometimes restrained with leather wrist and **ankle straps;** see also **C and R, restraints**

strats *cigarettes;* see **bif**

strawberry tablets *Ecstasy:* see **E**

stretch *sentence of 12 months imprisonment;* see also **calendar**

strip blanket used in a strip cell made of untearable material; see also **strip dress, paper suit, paper dress, space suit**

strip cell, strip *where a prisoner is confined 'in solitary' with only a mattress and cardboard chamber pot* meant to be used for violent or very disruptive prisoners until they are calmer; referred to as **in the strips;** see also **protected room, unfurnished room**

strip dress *garment made of untearable paper* worn in strip cell; see also **paper dress, space suit**

striper *prison weapon* made from a small brush with razor blades fixed into it. From the striped slashes it can inflict; see also **chiffy**

stripes *jeans* worn by people suspected of being likely to attempt escape and by some **Cat A** prisoners (from the yellow stripes on them); see also **blues, browns, E-List, E-man, patches, trotter, wallflower**

strippy *strip search* when coming from another prison, or from the visits area; see also **dry bath**

stripped cut with razor blades fixed into a small brush

strips see **block**

strip search see **dry bath, strippy**

strong box *cell used to hold disruptive prisoners* with special doors and usually no windows; see also **block**

strong it *face up to something/someone;* see also **front it**

stuff *drugs* usually hard drugs, especially cocaine (see **C**) and heroin (see **H**); also **hard stuff, good stuff**

sturmer *bad cheque;* see also **rubber cheque**

sub *'subversive' prisoner* who stirs up trouble; see also **jail politician, politician**

sugar see **LSD** (because it is sometimes taken on a sugar cube)

suicide kit *officers on night patrol may carry a pouch containing* e.g. scissors, rubber gloves and resuscitation equipment

suicide watch *officers looking in on a prisoner at risk of committing suicide* they will check at least every 15 minutes; see also **bed watch, POL I, special watch, SSS**

suit *an official visitor not in uniform;* see also **civvy**

sulph *amphetamine sulphate (speed)* in powder form: see **A**

supergrass *informer on major crime,* or may simply be highly prolific with information: see **grass**

supermans see **LSD**

Supermax *maximum security jail in the USA.* The Penitentiary Administrative Maximum Facility is the official title for the first Federal prison purpose built. Opened in November 1994 in the Colorado Rockies, it is known to staff as 'ADX' and to the public as 'Supermax'. It holds criminals in almost total seclusion. It replaced Marion, Illinois, as the highest security USA prison. The **Learmont Report** recommended a comparable prison for the UK

superweed see **marijuana** From the US fictional comic, film and TV character Superman

sus (1) *arrest on suspicion of a crime* (2) short for **suspect, suspicious, suspiciously** (3) *the so called 'sus law'* under which people could be stopped and search by police 'on suspicion'. Also **sussed** *observed or uncovered illegal activity;* see also **clocked**

111

swagged off *locked away* i.e. a prisoner's possessions; see also **disclaimer form, two box system, volumetrics**

sweatbox *prisoner transport* involving small individual cubicles: see **Black Maria**

sweats *suffered during withdrawal from drug addiction*

Sweeney *police* (rhyming slang: *Sweeney Todd = squad*). A label reinforced by the ITV fictional detective series *The Sweeney*; specifically used for the Metropolitan Police **Flying Squad,** but may also be used to refer to police from **Regional Crime Squads** and the proposed National Crime Squad (1996); see also **bill, brains, lying squad**

sweet *OK* all right

sweetener *bribe:* see **backhander**

swift *corrupt* (of police)

swift one *false arrest*

swing/swinger a way of transferring goods and contraband items from one cell to another: usually a plastic carrier bag on a long string, often made of torn pieces of sheet knotted together. The prisoner will let down the bag through the cell window and swing it across outside so another prisoner in a nearby cell can pull it in through his or her own window. Possibly found next morning in the yard if the prisoner is interrupted; see also **flying pasty, lines**

swinger *prisoner who attempts suicide* i.e. by hanging; see also **topped**

SWIP *shared working in prisons* the system whereby prison officers and seconded probation staff work together

swoop *raid* **swoop squad/team** *team specially trained and equipped to locate drugs and other contraband;* see also **squat team, cell spin, twirl**

swooper *someone who picks up cigarette-ends from the prison floor* i.e. to re-roll into new cigarettes; see also **dog-ender**

system *music system* usually an in-car stereo: 'I got done for nicking a system'; see also **Brixton briefcase, ghetto blaster, talking handbag, rad**

systems kicker *rebellious prisoner*

T

tab (1) *cigarette* see **bif.** (2) *small square of blotting paper* about a quarter of the size of a standard postage stamp, on which **acid** (see **LSD**) comes; see also **blotter** and **drop tabs.** Tabs come in many different designs and each name may derive from the printed motif (e.g. a cartoon character). Tabs are swallowed. The effect is called a **trip.** (3) *tablet* lawful or unlawful

TAC *temporary allocation centre*

tack see **marijuana**

tackle *heroin:* see **H**

take care of *wipe out by killing;* see also **take out**

take it Nelson *relax* take it (nice 'n) easy

take off *inject drugs*

take-off artist *escaped prisoner:* see **away**

take out *wipe out by killing* (derived from a US military expression); see also **take care of**

take the rap *take the blame* for someone else's crime

take the piss *urine test;* see also **MDT, piss test**

talking handbag *radio;* see also **Brixton briefcase, ghetto blaster, talking handbag, rad, sounds**

tally *prisoners count* (e.g. after **first unlock,** mealtimes or in the evening); see also **muster**

tangerine dreams, tangoes *Ecstasy:* see **E**

taps *blows in a fight;* see also **smacks**

tar *opium;* see **O**

tariff *minimum term* i.e. the part of a life sentence prisoner's sentence which must be served for 'retribution and deterrence'. At the end of the tariff period the prisoner can be released on licence if (a) the Home Secretary accepts a Parole Board recommendation for release of a *mandatory* life sentence prisoner or (b) the Parole Board directs the release of a *discretionary* life sentence prisoner.

task *masturbation;* see also **cell task**

taste *minute quantity of narcotics*

taxing (1) *bullying, extortion* of protection money or tobacco in prison. (2) *snatching valuables from passing cars* e.g. at traffic lights by opening the passenger door and stretching inside, especially where the driver is a vulnerable victim

taylors/tailors *bought cigarettes* as opposed to **roll-ups** (tailormade = factory made); see also **bif, salmon**

TDA *taking and driving away a vehicle* the modern offence of taking a conveyance under Theft Act 1968 replaced the former offence of taking and driving away, but the old description lingers on in common speech

tea see **marijuana.** Also **tea-head** someone who uses **marijuana**

tea boat when several prisoners club together to pay for tea: see also **brew, cup of diesel**

tealeaf *thief* (rhyming slang)

team *gang* **team-handed** *working in a gang*

tearup *very violent fight*

teaspoon *measure of heroin:* see **H**

telegram *written notice telling a prisoner he or she is on report* for an offence against **GOAD**; see also **on report, Rule 47**

telephone numbers *large sums of money* (implying five, six or seven figures)

temporary release/temporary licence the old temporary release and home leave schemes have been replaced by a new system called **release on temporary licence.**There are three types of licence: **compassionate licence, facility licence** and **resettlement**

113

licence. Each form of licence has different rules and all of them depend on prisoners passing a **risk assessment.** Some categories of prisoner are not eligible for any form of temporary licence, e.g. **Cat A** prisoners and those on the **E-List;** prisoners who are unconvicted or convicted but not sentenced; those subject to extradition procedures and those awaiting further charges. A **Cat B** prisoner cannot apply for a facility licence. All opportunities have been substantially reduced following changes in the rules governing temporary release imposed by the Home Secretary since 1995

t e m s *Temazepam* the drug benzodiazepine. Used in the short term treatment of insomnia or as an anti-depressant. Sold at raves for use in the **chill out room.** Cost £1.50 to £5 each. Green or yellow egg shaped capsules or white tablets. Other common names include **downers, eggs, green eggs, jellies, wobbly eggs**

Terrence Higgins Trust London-based charity providing advice, information and support on all matters associated with HIV/AIDS

Thai, Thailand grass see **marijuana**

Thaisticks two thin twigs wrapped around with **marijuana**

Thatchers *Ecstasy:* **see E.** After Margaret Thatcher, a former prime minister

thins *keys;* see also **pass key, spanners, twirl**

third degree *heavy questioning, harsh interrogation;* see also **strap**

THL *terminal home leave* last home leave before a prisoner is released

THT see **Terence Higgins Trust**

three day chop sudden reduction/total removal of drugs or drugs substitute; see also **juice, meth, reducing script**

three-ing, three up *three prisoners to a cell*

three moon *three month sentence:* see **carpet**

Threes *third landing in prison* this may be the highest landing, both physically and in **GOAD** terms. It can be a privilege in certain prisons to be housed on the Threes, and prisoners considered the least trouble are often allocated there. Sometimes used as an incentive; see also **Ones, Twos, Fours, Fives. IEPS**

three-sixties *360 degree turn* in joyriding

three stretch *three years in jail* (a **stretch** is one year)

throughcare the Prison Service has an official commitment to care for prisoners during their incarceration and to arrange for this to continue on release. This is stated in 'Framework for the Throughcare of Offenders' which emphasises that throughcare is a shared responsibility for Prison Service staff, voluntary organizations, the Probation Service and the offender himself or herself. Throughcare starts with **sentence planning**, continues through the sentence and is then handed on to the agency supervising a prisoner released on **licence**

throw the book at someone *prefer the maximum charge, or number of charges* i.e. 'everything in the book', or *mete out the maximum punishment*

thrust *amyl nitrite:* see **hardcore**

trades instructor someone who teaches a trade or skill in prison

TICs *taken into consideration* there is a well-established though non-statutory practice whereby a defendant may ask that outstanding offences for which he or she has not been prosecuted be taken into consideration when sentence is passed. The offences must be admitted. This is a means of 'clearing the slate' and making a clean breast of matters, and disposing of possible further cases quickly and easily

ticket *search warrant;* see also **W**

tie off *prepare a vein for a drugs injection;* see **main, mainline, tracking. Tie-up** the cord etc. used for this purpose; see also **rope**

tik *potential victim* (West Indian in origin)

time *period served in prison* Encapsulated in the age-old saying 'If you can't do the time, don't do the crime!'; see also **bird, bit, cons, lagging, porridge**

'time . . .' shops the trading name of shops selling goods made by prisoners and administered by the Prison Charity Shops Trust, often in tourist areas. Profits go to charity

time back if a prisoner has had days added because of breach of prison discipline (see **ADA**), he or she can apply to **the Board of Visitors** to get this **time back** and may be successful if more recent behaviour has been good

time through the gate *experience* officer slang for the time they have spent in the Prison Service

times two *double sentence* 'I got life times two.' May be **concurrent** or **consecutive**

TO/turnover unannounced search of cell; see also **cell spin, room spin, spin, swoop, twirl**

TOB *tackling offending behaviour* TOB groups are often run by probation officers and/or psychologists

TOIL *time off in lieu* In 1987, as a result of disputes and **POA** protests against staff cuts and financial cutbacks in the Prison Service, the Home Office carried out a review of prison staffing and management. A new approach based on **unified grades** was established and this initiative was called **Fresh Start.** The main change was the limiting of the number of hours worked each week by prison officers. This substantially reduced overtime. Officers were told they could take 'time off in lieu'

toke (1) *puff, inhale smoke* (of a **marijuana** cigarette): 'toke some grass'. (2) a **marijuana** cigarette; see also **bif, bifta**

tom (1) *prostitute* (2) *jewellery* (rhyming slang *tomfoolery = jewellery*)

tom squad, tom patrol *police who target prostitution*

ton *£100*

115

tool *weapon*

tooled up *carrying a weapon*

tool loss see **implement loss**

toot (1) a **line** (**snort**) of cocaine: see **C**; also the practice of smoking heroin by inhaling it from tin foil: see **H**. See also **boot, line, whistle**. (2) sniff, snort cocaine. (3) money, booty, loot (multiple rhyming slang *whistle and flute = toot = loot*).

toothbrush day when a convicted prisoner is sentenced

topped (self) *committed suicide;* see also **swinger**

torch *commit arson*

total bang up *in cells 24 hours a day;* see also **bangup, shutdown**

total wreck *cheque* (rhyming slang)

toting carrying prisoners to and from court in a cubicled van: see **Black Maria**

tout (1) *IRA informer* (2) *ticket tout*

town visit now called a community visit

tracking *injecting drugs into a vein;* see also **mainline, rope, tie off, tie up**. Also **tracks** *marks made by drugs needles*

trade *prostitution* (heterosexual or homosexual, but usually meaning the latter within prison); see also **rough trade**

tramp's lagging *prison sentence of 90 days;* see also **beggar's lagging, carpet, sorrowful tale, spell, three moon, tray**

tranks, tranx *tranquilizers* including Valium, Librium etc; see also **vallies**

transfer *movement of a prisoner from one prison to another;* see also **ghosted, shipped, transport**

travel warrant on release a prisoner is handed a warrant to cover his or her travel home or to where he or she will live; see also **discharge grant**

tray *three month sentence* probably from the french *trois* for *three*: see **carpet**

TRF *temporary release failure* when a prisoner misbehaves or **absconds** when on temporary release; see **home leave**

treatments *area where medication is handed out*

tree, off your tree, out of your tree *crazy* high on alcohol or drugs

trip drugs trip, usually meaning on LSD. Also **tripper, triphead** someone who uses LSD; **tripping** using LSD

triple Xs *Ecstasy:* see **E**

trolley route *route taken by food trolleys.* This is often the main thoroughfare that goes right round the prison; see also **cobitis, mucktruck**

trotter escaped prisoner; see also **cop a heel, E-list, E-man, over the fence, on the lam, over the hill, take off artist, wallflower**

trusty prisoner entrusted with responsibilities; see also **orderly, red band**

116

tube *officer who listens in on prisoners' conversations:* see **screw**

tucked up *arrested;* see also **nicked**

tunes *Tuinal* a barbiturate sleeping pill which can be misused; see **barb/barbs**

turd burglar *male homosexual;* see **bent**

turf *territory* e.g. of a gang; see also **manor, patch**

2 for The Queen

turkeying *going 'cold turkey'* withdrawing from drugs/alcohol; see also **cold turkey**

turning tricks *prostitution;* see also **going case**

turn over (1) *stop and search* (by police); see also **sus**. (2) *attack and beat up*

turn around *persuade to inform* see also **Queen's evidence**

turtles see **LSD**. From the American cartoon characters, the 'Teenage Mutant Ninja Turtles'

twat mags girlie magazines

twenty-four seven *all the time* twenty-four hours a day, seven days a week

twenty-eight day lie-down system whereby a difficult or dangerous prisoner is moved around from one prison to another, never staying in any establishment for longer than 28 days; see also **magic roundabout, shared misery circuit**

twighlight nurse *member of the health care staff on evening duty*

twirl (1) *prison officer* (from old slang word for key): see **screw** (2) *turn round during a strip search* (3) *cell search;* also known as a **cell spin, room spin, spin, TO**

two *two year sentence*

two box system see **disclaimer, property box, volumetrics**

two for one *100 per cent interest;* see also **double back, double bubble, juicer, loan shark**

two for the Queen see **ADA**

'two, giz a' *share something two ways* e.g. a cigarette

twocking *taking without owner's consent* usually a vehicle: see **TDA,**

TWC. Also **twockers** *people who take a conveyance without consent* including, e.g. joyriders

two-ing, two-up *two prisoners sharing a cell*

Twos *second landing* often the middle landing in a prison where prisoners of 'average' behaviour are housed; see also **Ones, Threes, Fours, Fives**

two stripes *prison trainer* from the stripes on officers' uniforms; see also **Adidas, CIT, IO, SGO**

two to unlock see **four to unlock**

two's up! 'Save us two of your **roll-ups**!' If a prisoner asks another for 'twos' it means he or she wants to share something, usually a cigarette - or it may mean wanting to give the other a share; see also **'two, giz a'**

U

umbrella brigade *Special Branch*

unauthorized possession when a prisoner is found to have articles in his or her possession which are disallowed, or to have too great a quantity of something; see also **IP**

unconvicted *an unconvicted prisoner* in prison 'on remand' awaiting trial or sentence

unfit, to *to deem a prisoner medically unfit* e.g. to be disciplined, to work. A prisoner who is mentally ill may be said by a prison medical officer to be incapable of understanding or responding to Prison **Rules** and therefore unfit for a governor's **adjudication**. Also **unfitted** *deemed unfit*

unified grades the eight grades between a top ranking **governor** (grade 1) and a basic grade officer (grade 8); see also **governor grades**; see also **Fresh Start, TOIL**

uniform (1) most male prisoners have to wear a uniform. Female prisoners and remand prisoners can wear their own clothes (2) *prison officer:* see **screw**

units *prison phonecard* prisoners may ask/harass other prisoners to 'borrow some units' and debts can build up. The prison phonecard looks like a standard phonecard except that it has stamped across it the words FOR USE IN HM PRISONS ONLY. Phonecards/units are a form of prison currency. Used cards can be sold to phonecard enthusiasts for around 50p (1996). See also **green and friendly, phonecard, phonecard deal**

unlock when prisoners are let out of cells, e.g. 'at first unlock'

uppers *amphetamines (speed):* see **A**

up the stairs *on trial* usually meaning before a jury in the Crown Court i.e. the court 'upstairs' in the criminal courts hierarchy (and which may sometimes be reached by going upstairs from underground cells)

user *drug addict*

USI *unlawful sexual intercourse* with a girl under 16, or under 13: see also **jailbait**

UT *unauthorised taking* usually of a motor vehicle; see also **TWC, twocking**

UV *ultraviolet stamp* placed on the hand of a visitor to prison as a security measure

V

V *visit;* see also **VO**

VA *voluntary associate* prison visitor linked to the probation service who befriends prisoners and may try to help them on release; see also **SOVA**. Not to be confused with a member of **BOV** or **NAPV**

vag, on a *on a vagrancy charge*

vallie(s) *Valium* a trade name for diazepam, a lawful tranquilizer which can be misused. Comes in three colours and sizes: white (2mg), yellow (5mg), blue (10mg), costing £2-£5 each; see also **barbs, eggs, green eggs, jellies, tranx, wobbly eggs**. 'I was **vallied up**' *on Valium;* see also **tranx**

V and V *Visions and Values* aims whereby prisons are run. The following 'mission statement' can be seen on walls inside every prison:

> Her Majesty's Prison Service serves the public by keeping in custody those committed by the Courts.
>
> Our duty is to look after them with humanity and to help them lead law abiding lives in custody and after release

VC (1) *volumetric control:* see **volumetrics** (2) *visiting committee* predecessor of the **Board of Visitors**

veg prep *vegetable preparation*

veras *vice squad* (after Vera Vice, from vice versa); see also **vice**

verbal/verbals confession/alleged confession. Although called

119

'verbals', this usually refers to written statement containing oral responses to police questions. Sometimes used as a verb, i.e. 'I was verballed', this would signify that the prisoner alleged that a so-called confession (oral or written) was false. Traditionally, and especially before PACE and tape-recorded interviews, verbals came to mean what the police said an accused person said. Some examples were well-trodden, a fact crystallised in a classic phrase which has passed into the public domain: 'It's a fair cop, guv.'

VERS *Voluntary Early Retirement Scheme* the Prison Service scheme whereby prison officers can be retrained or transferred

vet *prison doctor* see **pill pusher, scablifter, SMO**

vice, the *Vice Squad;* see also **veras**

villain *anyone with a criminal record*

Ville, The *HMP Pentonville*

visits entitlement to visits varies according to the status of the prisoner: **unconvicted/remand** prisoners are entitled to a minimum of 90 minutes each week. A prison usually allows one short visit every weekday; **sentenced** prisoners are only entitled to 60 minutes a month minimum - two 30 minute visits every four weeks, though this can be increased at the Governor's discretion. There are variations to this rule according to whether a prisoner is on a **Basic, Standard** or **Enhanced** regime (see **IEPS**). Visiting a relative in prison for the first time can be a daunting experience. The process begins

with prisoner sending the prospective visitor a **visiting order** bearing the names of the visitor(s). Three adult visitors are allowed at any one visit and a prisoner's children can also attend. The VO has to be brought along. In closed prisons, visits now usually have to be booked in advance. Visitors need ID in the form of, e.g. a driving licence. All goods, gifts etc for the prisoner must be handed in to a **receiving officer** at the gate. In some prisons, flowers for prisoners have recently been banned unless ordered in advance from a local florist and delivered direct to the prison. This is because drugs have been found concealed in the stems. All visitors' possessions must be left in a locker, except for a small amount of money for the purchase of refreshments. Closed prisons often now require visitors to leave jackets, scarves etc in the locker, and to submit to a routine search with a scanner. If the prisoner wishes to hand out any goods to the visitor, this has to be arranged in advance through official channels; see also **assisted visits, APVU, children's visits, enhanced visits, HALOW, legal visits, reception VO, VOs, vizzo**

visitors' centre most prisons now provide waiting room facilities for visitors. These have information and sometimes refreshments available, WC, baby changing room and facilities for children. Provision nation-wide tends to be patchy

vitamins *drugs in pill form*

vizzo *visit*

VO *visiting order* a pass note which prisoners are allowed to send out to visitors enabling them to visit. Up to three adults are usually permitted to

120

visit as well as the prisoner's children, though in some prisons there are special days for **children's visits;** see also **PVO.** Convicted prisoners have to send a VO to a visitor in advance of the visit. VOs can be used for 28 days from when they are issued and only on the visiting days permitted by the prison. Visitors must hand VOs in to the officer on the prison **gate** and in many prisons an instant photograph is taken which will be used in future as a security pass. VOs are not usually required by people visiting prisoners on remand or for **legal visits** or from a minister of religion (such visitors can fill in a form at the gate). An **enhanced VO** is an extra visit allowed to a prisoner, usually limited to once every month

volley *verbal abuse*

vols *volunteers* prison officer slang. The number of officers required for the various shifts of duty. A notice will be put up in their office saying 'Vols required for ED', meaning 'number of officers required for evening duty'. Other abbreviations include 'L-A' = Late A shift. Volunteers are also requested in respect of other details; see also **dotached duty, detail**

volumetrics *volumetric control* **(VC)** prisoners are allowed to keep only a limited number of personal possessions in their cells. This quantity is measured by the volume of goods that will fit into two boxes of a specified size, plus one set of clothing, plus one 'outsize item'. The contents of one of the boxes has to be kept in the prison store, the contents of the other can stay in the prisoner's cell. This is to facilitate easier searching of cells for contraband goods, especially drugs; see also **disclaimer form,** **prop box, prop card, two box system**

VP *vulnerable prisoner* prisoner on Rule 43; see **Rule 43.** Also **VPU, VP wing** vulnerable prisoners' unit, i.e. for prisoners who may be in danger from other prisoners e.g because they are sex offenders or child molesters, or because they have got into debt to other prisoners. The other category of Rule 43 prisoners in a VPU can be those who are a danger to themselves through self-mutilation or attempted suicide; see also **hospital wing, nonce wing, Rule 43, zoo**

VTC *vocational training course*

VTU *voluntary testing unit* some prisons operate a separate unit of accommodation e.g. a wing or block, which offers enhanced privileges to prisoners living there in return for voluntary tests to show they are not taking drugs. These prisoners sign a compact with the prison authorities agreeing to this arrangement but if this is broken they return to normal accommodation and lose their privileges; see also **drug-free wing/zone, MDT**

W

W *(search) warrant;* see also **ticket**

wafer *cigarette or drugs paper;* see also **leaves, papers, Rizlas, skins**

wages prisoners are paid a small wage for work they do; the current average weekly wage is about £7, though in some prisons it can rise to around £20 (1996). Prisoners without a job are paid a flat rate allowance

waiting for the numbers prison officer term used when waiting for the go-ahead to unlock prisoners from their cells. This may be announced over the tannoy from the central control room and cannot be issued until all prisoners are accounted for; see also **CACS, control room, first unlock, muster, numbers**

wake-up *first morning drugs dose*

walk, to *to be acquitted* and walk free from court: 'I was expecting to walk today'

wall, go over the *escape:* see **away** Also **wallflower** *prisoner making escape plan;* see also **away, E-List, E-man, escape committee, legger, take off artist, trotter**

Wanno *HMP Wandsworth ;* see also **Wozzer**

warehoused *contained* kept in prison with no education, training etc.

warm *good* **warm at** *good at*

wash (1) *crack cocaine:* see **C, crack, rock, stone** (2) *launder money* through an apparently legitimate business; see also **front man, laundromat**

wash out, wash up *wash out cocaine* i.e. into **crack:** see generally **C**

watchdog member of the **Board of Visitors (BOV)**

wax me *sort me out a joint*

wax up *conceal evidence* from practice of **greasing up:** oiling the anus to accommodate contraband

goods, e.g. drugs or money, hidden in a **charger**, a small hollow cylinder; see also **bottling**

WD *weekdays*

WE *weekends*

wear it *take the blame* for someone else's crime

Wallflower   Marijuana

weasel *coat* (rhyming slang *weasel and stoat = coat*)

weed, the weed *cannabis:* see **marijuana** Also **weedhead** someone who uses **marijuana**

weekend *exceptionally short prison sentence;* see also **bed and breakfast, haircut, shit and a shave.** Also **weekender** someone who only uses drugs at weekends;

122

weekend habit *occasional use of a so-called recreational drugs* e.g. Ecstasy (see **E**)

weighed off *sentenced* by a court, or a prison governor at an **adjudication**

weight *a measure of drugs*

welfare *prison welfare unit* which assists, e.g. with family matters, future accommodation and work on release; a prison's in-house probation unit; see also **care bear**

Wendy house *association* i.e. when prisoners are allowed out of cells to meet others; see also **association, playtime.** Contrast **dolls' house**

whacky backy see **marijuana**

wheelman *getaway car driver;* see also **just in caser, skid artist, stoppo driver**

where the sun don't shine *the anus* where items may be hidden to avoid discovery during a strip search; see also **bottling; charger**

whistle (1) *inhale drugs from foil* (rhyming slang: *whistle and flute = toot);* see also **chase the dragon.** (2) *suit* (old rhyming slang: *whistle and flute = suit);*

white burgers *Ecstasy:* see **E**

white doves *Ecstasy:* see **E**

white dust *amphetamines (speed)* in powder form: see **A**

white light see **LSD**

whiteline fever *cocaine addiction:* see **C, line**

white nurse *morphine:* see **M**

white shit *cocaine:* see **C**

whiteshirt *senior prison officer;* see also **screwdriver, SO**

white stuff *morphine:* see **M**

whizz *amphetamines (speed):* see **A**

whizzer, whizz mob, the whizz *pickpocket(s);* see also **dipper, diver**

whodunnit *prison meat pie;* see also **cob, duff, muck truck, yellow peril, trolley route**

whore's nark *informer* a reversal of **Noah's Ark.** May mean informing to the police, or about police activities to a prostitute: see generally **grass**

wild prints *unidentified fingerprints;* see **dabs**

wind up *annoy, goad*

windsock *female contraceptive* e.g. Femidom

wing, on the wing *section of a prison.* Every wing has a number of prison officers and a **wing officer** or **landing officer** in charge

winged, to be *disciplined* called to account

WIP *Women In Prison* organization which works for female prisoners and keeps in close contact with them

wire up *to wire up illicitly to electricity* e.g. via the light switch of a cell; see also **in cell electrics**

WISH *Women In Special Hospitals* organization to help women in prison who have mental health problems

wobbly eggs *Temazepam:* see **tems.** See also **eggs, green eggs, jellies**

wolf, prison wolf *older homosexual;* see also **bent, queen, closet queen**

wombling *picking up litter* from TV series The Wombles of Wimbledon Common; see also **skiprats**

wonder veg see **magic mushrooms**; see also **mushies, shrooms**

Woodcock Report report by Sir John Woodcock following escapes from HMP Whitemoor in 1994

woodener *30 day sentence*

woofter *male homosexual* (rhyming slang = *poofter*): see **bent**

Woolf Report report by Lord Woolf following prison disturbances and a siege at HMP Strangeways in 1990

working out *working outside the prison* as part of a pre-release scheme; see also **PRES**

works (1)*drugs equipment* syringes etc; see also **fit, gear, kit, outfit.** Also **clean works** fresh needles for injecting. (2) *prison maintenance* prisoners may be allocated to working parties to maintain areas of the prison fabric and grounds. Sometimes prisoners can learn a trade or skill and gain qualifications.

world cups see **LSD**

Wozzer, the *HMP Wandsworth*

W P R C *Women Prisoners' Resource Centre* workers from this group visit all women's prisons to give advice and information about accommodation and other facilities to women returning to the London area. Also offers advice and support after release

wrap packet of drugs usually wrapped in a small piece of paper. Often heroin, worth £10 or £20: 1996 (see **H**) but the term is also commonly applied to amphetamines (see **A**); see also **bag, finger, joey, paper, scorebag**

write up *bad disciplinary report;* see also **black pen**

wrong 'un (1) *sex offender:* see **animal** (2) *informer:* see **grass** (3) *untrusted person* especially when used by prisoners of prison staff, or vice versa.

WRVS *Women's Royal Voluntary Service* which may help serve refreshments during **visits**

X

X-Files *Ecstasy:* see **E** after the cult American science fiction/futuristic TV series *The X-Files*

Xs *Ecstasy:* see **E**; see also **triple Xs**

Y

yard see **cell**

yard girls *women cleaners* (prisoners); also called **yardies**

Yard, the *Scotland Yard;* see also **Kremlin**

YC *youth custody* now replaced by young offender institution (**YOI**)

Yellow Book *Prisoners' Information Book* published by the Prison Reform Trust and HM Prison Service and updated annually. Should be issued to every prisoner on **reception** into prison

yellow peril *prison cake* coloured bright yellow; see also **cob, cobitis, duff, duffer, whodunnit**

yellow sheet *previous convictions* i.e. the written document showing these; see also **form, former, PC, previous, rap sheet, record**

ying yangs see **LSD**

YO *young offender*

YOI *young offender institution* for detainees under the age of 21; see also **DC, detainee**

young offender estate see **estate**

YP *young prisoner* older prisoners sometimes use these initials as an insult to suggest that another prisoner ought to grow up, act more maturely; see also **starred up**

Z

zap *amyl nitrite* an inhalant: see **hardcore**

zerozero *cannabis:* see **marijuana**

zig and zags see **LSD**

zombie medicine *tranquilizers;* see also **Largactil shuffle, muppet shuffle**

zonked *drugged up;* see also **out of my head, out of my skull**

zonker *heavy drug user*

zoo *vulnerable prisoners'* (see **VP**) wing where offenders on **Rule 43** are kept for their own safety (probably comes from **animals**, a derogatory name for sex offenders). See also **hospital wing, nonce wing, VPU**

zoot *marijuana cigarette:* see **spliff**

Some other Waterside Press Titles

CRIMINAL JUSTICE, CRIMINAL POLICY AND SENTENCING

Introduction to the Criminal Justice Process Bryan Gibson and Paul Cavadino. 'Rarely, if ever, has this complex process been described with such comprehensiveness and clarity': *Justice of the Peace*. (First reprint, 1997) ISBN 1 872 870 09 0. £12.00 plus £1.50 p&p

Introduction to the Magistrates' Court Bryan Gibson (Second edition) A clear outline and a *Glossary of Words, Phrases and Abbreviations* (750 entries). ISBN 1 872 870 15 5. £10.00 plus £1.50 p&p

Introduction to the Probation Service Anthony Osler. An overview, including a brief history and modern-day responsibilities ISBN 1 872 870 19 8. £10.00 plus £1.50 p&p

Transforming Criminal Policy Andrew Rutherford. Looks at 'Spheres of Influence' in the USA, The Netherlands and England and Wales in the 1980s. ISBN 1 872 870 31 7. £16.00 plus £1.50 p&p **Criminal Policy Series**

The Sentence of the Court: A Handbook for Magistrates Michael Watkins, Winston Gordon and Anthony Jeffries. Consultant Dr. David Thomas. Foreword by Lord Taylor, Lord Chief Justice. (Fourth reprint, 1996). ISBN 1 872 870 25 2. In use for magistrates' training in many parts of England and Wales. 'Excellent': *The Law*. £10.00 plus £1.50 p&p

A to Z of Criminal Justice Paul Cavadino (1997) ISBN 1 872 870 10 4. £19.50

Criminal Justice and the Pursuit of Decency Andrew Rutherford. 'By reminding us that, without "good men and women" committed to humanising penal practice, criminal justice can so easily sink into apathy and pointless repression, Andrew Rutherford has sounded both a warning and a note of optimism.': *Sunday Telegraph* ISBN 1 872 870 21 X. £12.00 plus £1.50 p&p

Handbook of Effective Community Programmes Edited by Carol Martin. Published in association with the Institute for the Study and Treatment of Delinquency (ISTD). (1997) ISBN 1 872 870 44 9. £10.00 plus £1.50 p&p

YOUNG PEOPLE AND CRIME

Introduction to the Youth Court incorporating *The Sentence of the Youth Court*. Winston Gordon, Michael Watkins and Philip Cuddy. Foreword by Lord Woolf, Master of the Rolls. Produced under the auspices of the Justices' Clerks' Society. ISBN 1 872 870 36 8. £12.00 plus £1.50 p&p

Children Who Kill Edited by Paul Cavadino. From the tragic Mary Bell and Jamie Bulger cases to events world-wide. Contributors include Gitta Sereny, Peter Badge, Dr. Norman Tutt and Dr. Susan Bailey. Published in conjunction with the British Juvenile and Family Courts Society (BJFCS). 'Highly recommended': *The Law* ISBN 1 872 870 29 5. £12.00 plus £1.50 p&p

Growing Out of Crime The New Era Andrew Rutherford. The classic and challenging work about young offenders. ISBN 1 872 870 06 6. £12.50 plus £1.50 p&p

Juvenile Delinquents and Young People in Trouble in an Open Environment Edited by William McCarney. An international survey of youth justice. Published in conjunction with the International Association of Juvenile and Family Court Magistrates (IAJFCM). ISBN 1 872 870 39 2. £18.00 plus £1.50 p&p

Introduction to the Scottish Children's Panel Alistair Kelly. The first basic book in 20 years on this topic. ISBN 1 872 870 38 4. £12.00 plus £1.50 p&p

SPECIAL INTEREST

Interpreters and the Legal Process Joan Colin and Ruth Morris. For all people who are interested in spoken language or sign language in the legal context. ISBN 1 872 870 28 7. £12.00 plus £1.50 p&p

Justice for Victims and Offenders Martin Wright (Second edition). A completely new and fully updated treatment of this highly regarded work. ISBN 1 872 870 35 X. £16.00 plus £1.50 p&p

Capital Punishment: Global Issues and Prospects Edited by Peter Hodgkinson and Andrew Rutherford. Deals with the topic world-wide. ISBN 1 872 870 32 5. £32.00 plus £1.50 p&p **Criminal Policy Series** 'This book will replace many other sources of information': *Justice of the Peace*

Relational Justice: Repairing the Breach Edited by Jonathan Burnside and Nicola Baker. Foreword by Lord Woolf. As featured in *The Guardian*. (1994) ISBN 1 872 870 22 8. £10.00 plus £1.50 p&p

Punishments of Former Days Ernest Pettifer (1992) 'A good read.': *The Magistrate* ISBN 1 872 870 05 8. £9.50 plus £1.50 p&p

I'm Still Standing Bob Turney. A prisoner autobiography which will be of interest to all people concerned about crime, punishment and offending (1997). ISBN 1 872 870 43 0. £12.00 plus £1.50 p&p

All the above books are available from Waterside Press, Domum Road, Winchester SO23 9NN Tel or fax 01962 855567. Cheques should be made payable to 'Waterside Press'. Please remember to add p&p

Also by Angela Devlin

Criminal Classes: Offenders at School

ISBN 1 872 870 30 9. £16.00 plus £1.50 p&p

What the critics said:

'A wise and absorbing volume: if you are in any doubt about the links between poor education, crime and recidivism, read it': Marcel Berlins *The Guardian*

'An extremely frank and interesting insight': Victoria Myerson *The Law*

'Somebody buy this book for John Major': Peter Kingston *The Guardian*

'A book of considerable public importance which calls for attention': Sir Stephen Tumim

Criminal Classes is available from Waterside Press, Domum Road, Winchester SO23 9NN Tel or fax 01962 855567. Cheques should be made payable to 'Waterside Press'. Please remember to add p&p

Prison Visits Training Pack

Prison visits are a vital part of the training of new magistrates and for experienced magistrates to keep them well informed about local facilities. To assist with this process the Magistrates' Association has produced a *Prison Visits Training Pack* (as mentioned in the introduction to *Prison Patter*). The pack is designed to be used for the organization and preparation of training visits by magistrates to penal institutions. Supported by the Prison Service, it contains information on the aims of prison visits, preparation, conducting the visit, feedback and a resource section.

The pack is available to members and other interested parties from The Magistrates' Association, 28 Fitzroy Square, London W1P 6DD, price £14.00 (post free). Cheques should be made payable to 'The Magistrates' Association'